Jesus' Last Days
BIBLICAL MEDITATIONS

Jesus' Last Days
BIBLICAL
MEDITATIONS

Most Rev. Arthur J. Serratelli
S.T.D., S.S.L., D.D.

CATHOLIC BOOK PUBLISHING CORP.
New Jersey

NIHIL OBSTAT: Rev. T. Kevin Corcoran, MA
Censor Librorum
IMPRIMATUR: ✠ Most Rev. David M. O'Connell, C.M., J.C.D., D.D.
Bishop of Trenton
November 1, 2018

The Nihil Obstat and Imprimatur are official declarations that a book or pamphlet is free of doctrinal or moral error. No implication is contained therein that those who have granted the Nihil Obstat and Imprimatur agree with the contents, opinions, or statements expressed.

Acts—Acts of the Apostles	Hb—Habakkuk	2 Kgs—2 Kings	2 Pt—2 Peter
	Heb—Hebrews	Lam—Lamentations	Rom—Romans
Am—Amos	Hg—Haggai	Lk—Luke	Ru—Ruth
Bar—Baruch	Hos—Hosea	Lv—Leviticus	Rv—Revelation
1 Chr—1 Chronicles	Is—Isaiah	Mal—Malachi	Sir—Sirach
2 Chr—2 Chronicles	Jas—James	1 Mc—1 Maccabees	1 Sm—1 Samuel
Col—Colossians	Jb—Job	2 Mc—2 Maccabees	2 Sm—2 Samuel
1 Cor—1 Corinthians	Jdt—Judith	Mi—Micah	Song—Song of Songs
2 Cor—2 Corinthians	Jer—Jeremiah	Mk—Mark	Tb—Tobit
Dn—Daniel	Jgs—Judges	Mt—Matthew	1 Thes—1 Thessalonians
Dt—Deuteronomy	Jl—Joel	Na—Nahum	
Eccl—Ecclesiastes	Jn—John	Neh—Nehemiah	2 Thes—2 Thessalonians
Eph—Ephesians	1 Jn—1 John	Nm—Numbers	
Est—Esther	2 Jn—2 John	Ob—Obadiah	Ti—Titus
Ex—Exodus	3 Jn—3 John	Phil—Philippians	1 Tm—1 Timothy
Ez—Ezekiel	Jon—Jonah	Phlm—Philemon	2 Tm—2 Timothy
Ezr—Ezra	Jos—Joshua	Prv—Proverbs	Wis—Wisdom
Gal—Galatians	Jude—Jude	Ps(s)—Psalms	Zec—Zechariah
Gn—Genesis	1 Kgs—1 Kings	1 Pt—1 Peter	Zep—Zephaniah

(T-932)

ISBN 978-1-947070-35-6

© 2019 by Catholic Book Publishing Corp.
77 West End Rd.
Totowa, NJ 07512
Printed in Canada
www.catholicbookpublishing.com

Table of Contents

Dedicated to
My Beloved Mother
Eva Serratelli
(1914-2014)

INTRODUCTION

Today it has become commonplace among biblical scholars to speak of the importance of the Passion narrative in the Gospel. Each gospel writer gathered stories and sayings of Jesus treasured in the Church's memory. Some of their material had already been committed to writing; some still circulated by word of mouth. The gospel writers adapted the material to their particular audience.

Mark wrote to Christians under persecution. His readers were living in Rome around the traumatic time of the Jewish War (66-70 A.D.). To these Christians in conflict, Mark addressed his message about the Messiah who suffered and died before entering His glory.

The author of Matthew's gospel designed his work for Jewish-Christians living in Syria, probably in Antioch, about 80-90 A.D. His readers were struggling with their separation from the synagogue and their new associations with Gentiles within the Christian community. The gospel writer encouraged them to see the Church as the true people of God formed by Jesus, the New Moses.

About the same time, Luke wrote to Gentile Christians who had some affiliation with the Church at Antioch. His readers were coming to include more and more influential converts and were facing the politics of the Roman Empire. Luke presents them with the message of salvation now offered to all, rich and poor, Jew and Gentile, through Jesus.

Most likely about 90-100 A.D., the fourth evangelist composed his gospel. Ephesus remains the most likely place of origin. The readers of this gospel were seriously engaged in defending their claims about Jesus against Jewish objections. The evangelist addressed them with a spiritual gospel. He explains the theology of Jesus as the Son of God and the only way of salvation in order to strengthen their faith.

Although each writer composed his gospel for different people and with different purpose, there is one striking similarity in their works. Each devotes much attention to the story of the Passion. A quick glance at the outline of the written gospels reveals how much space is given over to telling the suffering and death of Jesus. In fact, the narration of Jesus' final days represents such a large part of the gospel that the Passion may even seem unduly emphasized. This fact is important.

The gospel writers could not forget those days of Jesus' suffering. They write their gospels bathed in the light of Easter Sunday morning. It is the Lord risen from the dead and living among the community of believers that they proclaim. Yet the dark shadows of Good Friday still fall clearly across the pages of their gospels. The Passion Story never lost its enthralling fascination even for the evangelists who had heard it many times before.

CHAPTER 1

THE OPPOSITION OF JESUS' ENEMIES

The Pharisees went out and immediately took counsel with the Herodians against him to put him to death. (Mk 3:6)

A t no point of the year are the sunsets so beautiful as in the autumn. Before the dark of winter, nature unfolds her richest tints and fairest charms. The woods burst into bright colors and clouds display their spectacular transfiguration. The hidden beauty of fading flower and fleeting sunset stand unmasked at the very moment death claims them for its own.

So it is with the hidden beauty of Jesus in the first gospel ever written. It is only when the forces of evil throw their thick mantle across His life in the gospel of Mark that there burst forth the brightest truths and richest revelations of Jesus.

In the very first line of his gospel, Mark proclaims the mystery he is about to unravel throughout his gospel. He writes:

The beginning of the gospel of Jesus Christ, the Son of God. (1:1)

Jesus Christ, the Son of God! That truth is like a bud about to blossom on a springtime twig. It is a truth that unfolds gradually in the warm sun of

Jesus' Galilean ministry. As Jesus smashes the sovereignty of Satan, He is recognized as the Christ come to re-establish God's reign on earth. Yet, it is not until the sun sets on the Judean ministry of Jesus that the truth of His person flowers forth. Only when evening falls, is He seen as truly the Son of God.

The first scene in the gospel of Mark that reveals Jesus as God's Son is His baptism:

> *It happened in those days that Jesus came from Nazareth of Galilee and was baptized in the Jordan by John. On coming up out of the water he saw the heavens being torn open and the Spirit, like a dove, descending upon him. And a voice came from the heavens, "You are my beloved Son; with you I am well pleased."*
>
> (1:9-11)

Yet, no sooner does the Father's blessing fall on Jesus, the Son in whom He is pleased, than the Spirit drives Jesus into the desert. There He struggles with the devil.

Conflict, contradiction, and suffering: this is the first impression Mark gives us of Jesus in the world. And not without reason. Mark seems almost fascinated with the suffering of Jesus. No mere coincidence accounts for the fact that this first evangelist writes the shortest account of the life of Jesus but the longest account of His Passion. Nearly one-half of the gospel narrative he gives over to the telling of the suffering and death of Jesus.

Mark dwells so much on the events of the Passion for two very good reasons. First, he wishes to inject a bit of realism into the faith of the first Christians. These early believers were excited about the Resurrection and the Second Coming. They were so enthused about the return of Jesus in glory that they kept thinking of His power, majesty, and divinity. The evangelist would have them remember that it was through suffering Jesus came into His glory.

Second, Mark wishes to relate the actual situation of his readers to the life of the Master. They were facing the dark hour of persecution; and, the evangelist would have them remember that it was in darkness, not light, that Jesus suffered. It was in dedication to God's hidden will that Jesus passed to glory. The Christian must expect the same.

Conflict and suffering: this is the thread carefully holding the first gospel together. Jesus faces both the mounting hostility of His enemies and the deepening misunderstanding of His friends throughout His public ministry. The Cross casts its shadow over Jesus from the very beginning. Whether it be said of Jesus himself or every Christian, there is no crown-bearer in heaven who has not been a cross-bearer on earth.

In Mark's gospel, the mystery of Jesus unfolds with greater vividness as His suffering increases. In the first half of the gospel, Jesus faces opposition from His enemies and reveals the very power of God. He expels demons with a word. He silences the Pharisees with the truth. According to Mark, the very first miracle takes place in the synagogue of Capernaum where Jesus is confronted by a demoniac (Mk 1:21-27).

Certainly, a house of worship is a strange place to find a devil. But all of us, like this man, come into the presence of God in need of being freed from oppression. When the demon sees Jesus, he cries out:

> *What have you to do with us, Jesus of Nazareth? Have you come to destroy us?*
>
> (Mk 1:24a)

It is the terrible cry of the doomed. The demon recognizes that the opposition is too strong. He is aware of the threat to his power in the person and teaching of Jesus. He begins by speaking with the plural pronoun "us," referring to all the other forces of evil that conspire with him against God. Jesus is indeed a menace to all evil.

> *Speaking for himself, the demon then says, "I know who you are, the Holy One of God."*
>
> (Mk 1:24)

He recognizes Jesus as the Messiah. As James reminds us, *"Even the demons believe…and tremble"* (Jas 2:19). There is no heresy in hell. With the sharp command, "Quiet, come out of him" (Mk 1:25), Jesus casts out the demon. The battle between Him and the forces of evil is now in the open.

After rounding off the first chapter with a series of cures (Mk 1:29-45), the evangelist strings together a series of controversies which Jesus has with His adversaries (Mk 2:1—3:6). Jesus cures the paralytic, eats with sinners, and discusses the practice of fasting. In the eyes of the Pharisees, Jesus breaks the Sabbath rest when He allows His disciples to pluck corn on a Sabbath and when He performs a healing miracle on a Sabbath. With each new episode, the opposition to Jesus mounts. Yet in each instance, Jesus muzzles His opponents with a word.

So strong is the hostility to Jesus that His enemies begin to plot His death:

> *The Pharisees went out and immediately took counsel with the Herodians against him to put him to death.* (Mk 3:6)

Mark is giving a first impression of Jesus to temper the enthusiastic faith of his readers. Jesus is the invincible worker of miracles, the unforgettable teacher of truth. Jesus has tremendous success. Yet, His enemies do not become His friends. In fact, they begin to plot against Him at the beginning of His public ministry.

*The men were amazed and asked,
"What kind of man is this? Even the
winds and the sea obey him!"*
(Mt 8:27)

CHAPTER 2

THE MISUNDERSTANDING OF JESUS' FRIENDS

*What I am doing, you do not understand now,
but you will understand later.* (Jn 13:7)

In the first half of Mark's gospel, Jesus is the target of His enemies' murderous designs. In the second half of the gospel, the atmosphere changes. Jesus now becomes the victim of His friends' misunderstandings. Jesus is found in the white heat of conflict with His friends and cruelty from His foes. And like gold tested in fire (Sir 2:1-5), He proves His worth. He is seen as God's Son.

While some people may lean wholly on human support and others turn only to God, Jesus depended both on the support of His friends and the assistance of His Father. He needed both as He faced the world's loneliest battle against evil. On so many occasions, Jesus' friends do not understand Him.

After Jesus calms the storm at sea, His disciples are confused. They do not know what to make of Jesus.

*They were filled with great awe and said to
one another, "Who then is this whom even
wind and sea obey?"* (Mk 4:41)

On another occasion, when Jesus comes walking to them on the water, they do not recognize Him.

They had just witnessed the multiplication of the loaves; yet, they still do not understand who Jesus is (Mk 6:45-52).

The first time that Jesus begins to speak of His impending suffering, they fail to follow His thought (Mk 8:31-33). They even fear to question Him any further (Mk 9:30-32). When Jesus warns them at the Last Supper that they are about to abandon Him, they do not understand. Each of them protests and promises death rather than denial (Mk 14:26-31). So thick has their misunderstanding become that Jesus' closest friends, Peter, James and John, sleep during the Agony in the Garden. And not even Jesus' repeated pleas can rouse them. So dark has their misunderstanding become that it blackens into failure.

Others have opposed Jesus because they do not want to lose their petty kingdom. His own oppose Him because they do not understand that they will gain the kingdom of God only through suffering.

It is an interesting fact recorded in the Scriptures that the greatest obstacles to God's work come not so much from His enemies but from His friends. After his exile from home, Jacob has to be taught his dependence on God before he returns to the land of promise. Jacob had cheated his brother Esau of his birthright as firstborn. Jacob is now heir to the promises made to Abraham. As Jacob is about to re-enter the promised land, he imagines that Esau is about to kill him. His death at the hands of his own brother would end the promises made to Abraham. But, Esau is no longer hostile. He welcomes his brother Jacob. The real threat to God's fulfilling His promises is not the hostility of Esau. It is Jacob's own lack of trust in God (Gen 32). There is much in this world that God can accomplish if we, His chosen instruments, depended more on Him in trust and love.

And he said to them, "Thus it is written that the Messiah would suffer and rise from the dead on the third day…"

(Lk 24:46)

CHAPTER 3

GOD'S SALVIFIC PLAN

For God so loved the world that he gave his only Son, so that everyone who believes in him might not perish but might have eternal life.

(Jn 3:16)

Throughout the account of the final days of Jesus' life, there are many scriptural references. They are essential to the narrative. In fact, the many citations and allusions to Scripture are like the pieces of a mosaic, giving the image its beauty and depth.

When Jesus enters Jerusalem for the last week, He comes as the humble Messiah-King seated on a donkey as Zechariah had predicted (Zech 9:9). When Jesus goes to pray in the Garden of Gethsemane, He himself voices the prophecy of Zechariah 13:7:

I will strike the shepherd, and the sheep will be dispersed. (Mk 14:27)

In His response to the high priest's questioning before the Sanhedrin, Jesus solemnly attests to His divinity by combining Daniel 7:13 and Psalm 110:1:

....you will see the Son of Man seated at the right hand of the Power and coming with the clouds of heaven. (Mk 14:62)

Jesus' statement at the Last Supper that someone at table with Him is about to betray Him (Mk 14:18) echoes the doleful sigh of the psalmist:

Even my trusted friend, who ate my bread, has raised his heel against me. (Ps 41:10)

And, Jesus' final prayer on the Cross (Mk 15:34) repeats the cry of the psalmist:

My God, my God, why have you abandoned me? (Ps 22:1)

In many places in the Passion narrative, the Old Testament is not directly cited but the language of the Old Testament is evoked. For example, Jesus' guarded silence during His interrogation before both the Jewish and Roman authorities (Mk 14:61 and 15:5) resembles the silence of the Suffering Servant of Isaiah:

Though harshly treated, he submitted and did not open his mouth. Like a lamb led to slaughter or a sheep silent before shearers, he did not open his mouth. (Is 53:7)

Likewise, many of the details of the Passion narrative are framed in the language of the Old Testament. The offer of wine to Jesus on the Cross (Mk 15:36), evokes the lament of the just man falsely accused:

Insult has broken my heart, and I despair; I looked for compassion, but there was none, for comforters, but found none. Instead they gave me poison for my food; and for my thirst they gave me vinegar. (Ps 69:21-22)

The dividing of Jesus' garments by lots recalls the ill treatment of the psalmist:

They divide my garments among them; for my clothing they cast lots. (Ps 22:19)

The taunts of the wicked around the Cross repeat those against the virtuous man in Wisdom 2:10-20 (Mk 15:29-32). And, the very death of Jesus crucified between two criminals (Mk 15:27) recalls the fate of the Suffering Servant:

He was given a grave among the wicked, a burial place with evildoers. (Is 53:9)

Even the darkness that covers the earth from noon to three in the afternoon at the moment of Jesus' death recalls Amos' prophecy of the Day of the Lord:

"And on that day," says the Lord God, "I will make the sun go down at noon and darken the earth in broad daylight." (Amos 8:9)

All these scriptural allusions are hardly coincidental. Each detail of the Passion from Jesus' entry into Jerusalem amid the cheering crowd to His exit from the same city amid a jeering rabble to His ignominious death on Golgotha is supported by the Scriptures. The constant weaving of Old Testament passages into so many details of the Passion narrative is meant to tell us that everything that is happening in the suffering and death of Jesus is taking place by God's design. Jesus' death is not an accident of history.

Furthermore, the careful attention to the timing of each moment of the Passion narrative reinforces the fact that everything is moving along according to a preordained schedule. When Jesus is being questioned by the Sanhedrin and Peter denies Jesus, Mark notes,

> *And immediately the cock crowed a second time.* (14:72)

When Jesus is bound and led to Pilate, Mark notes that this happens *"as soon as morning came"* (15:1). When Jesus is crucified, Mark tells us that *"it was nine o'clock in the morning"* (15:25). And, according to Mark, precisely at three o'clock in the afternoon, the heavens, as if in horror, hide their face, darkness covers the land and Jesus dies (15:33-34). Mark also notes that the burial of Jesus took place in the evening (15:42) and His Resurrection very early in the morning (16:2).

This close observation of the exact time of the events of Jesus' Passion is significant. It is the evangelist's way of putting the events on a schedule. He is telling us nothing happens by chance. With each hour ticking away, God's will is being accomplished.

Throughout the Passion story, the first evangelist takes pains to emphasize this truth: the Father wills the Cross. It is God who wills the best of men to suffer the worst of fates. The Cross is God's plan for our salvation.

Beneath all the events of the Passion is the God who loves us and wills to redeem us. Judas conspires with Jesus' enemies to hand Him over to them (Mk 14:10). He leaves the Last Supper to hand Jesus over (Mk 14:21). And, in the Garden of Gethsemane, Jesus is betrayed or handed over (Mk 14:41). Ultimately, not being able to impose the sentence of death, the Jews hand Jesus over to Pilate (Mk 15:1). But, beneath all of these events of "handing over," Jesus is the saving action of the Father. As Paul teaches,

God...did not spare his own Son but handed him over for us. (Rom 8:32)

Ultimately, it is the Father who wills the Cross.

He said to them, "I have eagerly
desired to eat this Passover with you
before I suffer, for, I tell you, I shall not
eat it again until there is fulfillment in
the kingdom of God."

(Lk 22:15-16)

CHAPTER 4

MASTER OF HIS OWN DESTINY

This is why the Father loves me, because I lay down my life in order to take it up again. No one takes it from me, but I lay it down on my own. (Jn 10:17-18)

The events of the Passion are not haphazard. They occur as they have been planned. As the final week of His life begins, Jesus approaches Jerusalem and instructs two of His disciples:

Go into the village opposite you, and immediately on entering it, you will find a colt tethered on which no one has ever sat. Untie it and bring it here. If anyone should say to you, "Why are you doing this?" reply, "The Master has need of it and will send it back here at once." So they went off and found a colt tethered at a gate outside on the street, and they untied it. Some of the bystanders said to them, "What are you doing, untying the colt?" They answered them just as Jesus had told them to, and they permitted them to do it. (Mk 11:1-6)

Jesus' actions are deliberately dramatic. He is acting out the prophecy about the king who will come and inaugurate a reign of peace:

Exult greatly, O daughter Zion!
Shout for joy, O daughter Jerusalem!
Behold: your king is coming to you,
a just savior is he,
Humble, and riding on a donkey,
on a colt, the foal of a donkey. (Zech 9:9)

Thus, as Jesus, enters Jerusalem, He is presenting himself as that king who brings a peace that the world cannot know of itself (Jn 14:27). Through His suffering, death and resurrection, He reconciles us to the Father and to one another. As Paul says, Jesus *"is our peace"* (Eph 2:14).

In His triumphant entrance into Jerusalem as the royal Messiah of peace, Jesus is presenting himself as the long-awaited Messiah. He plans everything and everything happens according to His plan. He prophesies to His own disciples what will take place and His prophecy is fulfilled.

Similarly, in arranging for the Last Supper, Jesus sends two disciples with precise instructions:

On the first day of the Feast of Unleavened Bread, when they sacrificed the Passover Lamb, his disciples said to him, "Where do you want us to go and prepare for you to eat the Passover?" He sent two of his disciples and said to them, "Go into the city and a man will meet you, carrying a jar of water. Follow him. Wherever he enters, say to the master of the house, 'The Teacher says, "Where is my guest room where I may eat the Passover with my disciples?"' Then he will show you a large upper room furnished and ready. Make the preparations for us there." The disciples then went off, entered the city, and found it just as he had told them; and they prepared the Passover. (Mk 14:12-16)

In Jesus' day, it would be quite unusual for a man to fetch the water. Jesus meets a Samaritan woman, not a man, drawing water from the well. Thus, it is very easy for the disciples to spot the man about whom Jesus speaks. They could not fail to notice a man doing a woman's work and carrying a vessel of water. Perhaps, the man may even have been a disciple of Jesus. Even our smallest, ordinary tasks can serve the Master. All that happens takes place just as Jesus predicts.

In both the preparation for His triumphant entrance into Jerusalem and the celebration of the Last Supper, Jesus manifests foreknowledge of what will take place. He knows what is to unfold even to the smallest detail. Everything happens as He orders it. Certainly, the Passion comes as no surprise to Him. He is in control. As He tells His disciples at the Last Supper:

I lay down my life in order to take it up again. No one takes it from me, but I lay it down on my own. I have power to lay it down, and power to take it up again. (Jn 10:17-18)

History is at His service. He is the master of His own destiny. He knows the Father's will. Both His life and His words say to the Father *"Thy will be done on earth, as it is in heaven"* (Mt 6:10).

CHAPTER 5

THE GARDEN OF GETHSEMANE

Then Jesus came with them to a place called Gethsemane. (Mt 26:36)

In the garden of Paradise, Adam and Eve fell from grace. In the Agony in the Garden, the new Adam rose to glory. Hiding in shame from the face of God, our first parents stood in fear. Exposed to the will of the Father, Jesus lay prostrate in agony. Eden and Gethsemane tell the story of communion with God. Eden speaks of a man and a woman united in sin and separated from God. Gethsemane speaks of a single man apart from His friends, yet one with God.

When the first evangelist came upon the story of the Passion, he decided to introduce new material to alert his readers to the tragedy and the triumph of Jesus' suffering. He skillfully arranged his account so that the reader might both grope in the darkness and walk in the light of the Cross. Mark's account of the Last Supper ends on a joyful note:

Then, after singing a hymn, they went out to the Mount of Olives. (14:26)

Jesus is serenely confident of His mission. He sings. It is hardly without significance that this is the only place in the gospel story where we are told Jesus sang. The moment is right.

Celebrating the Passover, Jesus is singing the words of the great Hallel (Ps 115-118). These psalms commemorate the exodus of the Jews out of Egypt into the Promised Land. Now on the lips of Jesus, these psalms celebrate humankind's journey from the slavery of sin to the freedom of grace as Jesus passes over from death to the life of the resurrection. In the Passover of the Hebrews, one nation moved from death to life. In the Passover of Jesus, all peoples pass to new life. No wonder Jesus sings.

As the last joyful note falls silent, Jesus makes His way to the Mount of Olives. The flickering lights of the Upper Room give way to the shadows of the night, as joy turns to sorrow and the Master enters His agony. Mark carefully tells the story of the Agony in the Garden at this point so that the reader feels the pathos of a suffering Jesus. Jesus is confident. Yes! But His confidence costs Him dearly.

The Mount of Olives is freighted with history. It is the very spot that once witnessed the tears of King David. David, revered for his victories, famed for his prowess, came to this spot, distraught at the rebellion of his son Absalom, whom he loved so much. Barefoot and broken, David reached the summit of the mount and threw himself prostrate before God. With sighs and lamentations, he wailed and wept aloud (2 Sam 15:30). On the slopes of the same mount, Jesus, the Son of David, suffers for all God's rebellious sons and daughters. So great is Jesus' anguish that *"his sweat became like drops of blood falling on the ground"* (Lk 22:44).

Mark gives two names to the place of Jesus' agony. He calls it the Mount of Olives and Gethsemane. According to Zechariah 14:4, when the end-time came, the Lord would position himself on this spot to win victory over His people's enemies. Mark would have us keep in mind that this moment of Jesus' entering the Mount of Olives begins that final struggle of history.

In fact, Mark emphasizes this with Jesus' first words to Peter, James, and John: *"remain here, and keep watch"* (14:34). In Mark's gospel, Jesus had ended His discourse about the end-time with a three-fold repetition of the same word "watch" or "stay awake" (13:33, 35, 37). Now He reports the same admonition. The point is clear. In the garden, Jesus is beginning the final hour. It is the beginning of the end times. The disciples indeed fall asleep during the Agony in the Garden (14:37), but Mark would have us stay awake and watch. For from the ruins of the old world, the new world is being made. These are truly the last days.

Second, Mark locates the place of Jesus' agony in "Gethsemane" (14:32). Gethsemane is a three-quarters-of-a-mile walk from the walls of Jerusalem across the Kedron Valley. It was a place filled with olive trees. During the Passover, Jerusalem's normal population of 40,000 would swell to over 150,000 people. Jesus had often come to this place before (Jn 18:2). So, on the night before He dies, He comes with His disciples to this secluded garden, filled with happy memories. The disciples are heavy with sleep from their Last Supper celebration. As on previous Passovers, they expect to find peace beneath the quiet olive trees.

The garden takes its name from an oil press on the property: "Gethsemane" means "oil press." Oil was used to anoint kings. The Messiah is the Anointed One. Now, in this garden where olives are pressed into oil, Jesus the Messiah is pressed into total abandonment to the Father's will and it is painful. In the grip of an unfathomable agony, Jesus is crushed; and, from His suffering, there comes forth the most precious oil to heal the world's wounds. As the Passover moon shines bright in the heavens above, Jesus undergoes the darkest hour in the depths of His soul. Humanity is being re-formed in the image that God intends.

CHAPTER 6

THE FINAL TEST

And he began to feel sorrow and distress. Then he said to them, "My soul is sorrowful even to death." (Mt 26:37-38)

In His instruction to the three apostles accompanying Him in His prayer in the Garden of Gethsemane, Jesus exhorts them to pray that they not *"undergo the test"* (Mk 14:38). This is the final hour of testing. This is the trial that must take place before God's reign is established on earth.

Jesus had already faced "temptation" or "testing" before this moment. In fact, this present struggle in the garden at the end of Jesus' ministry runs parallel to the testing in the desert at the start of His ministry (Mk 1:12-13; Mt 4:1-11; Lk 4:1-13). In the desert, He had struggled to reject the suggestion of Satan to accomplish His mission. Now, in the garden, He struggles to accept the last details of the Father's plan for redemption.

Mark records the intensity of that struggle with one of the most revealing sentences of his gospel:

And he began to be troubled and distressed.

(14:33)

The Greek words that Mark uses to say "to be troubled" and "to be distressed" express the strongest emotions. Jesus' first feeling is one of terrified surprise. He is shocked. This cannot be true. He then becomes anguished when He realizes it is. The boldness of these words is startling. The author of Matthew's gospel weakens Mark's description (Mt 26:37). Luke deletes it completely. But Mark would not have us miss the intense pain Jesus experienced in Gethsemane.

So great is Jesus' distress that, after saying *"my soul is very sorrowful even to death"* (Mk 14:34), Jesus falls on the ground and prays (Mk 14:35). The Greek verb does not simply mean that He prayed. Rather, it carries the idea of repeated petition. More exactly, Mark is telling us that Jesus prays and prays and prays.

Nowhere else but here in Mark do we see Jesus prostrate in the utter dejection of human nature. This is no empty show. Jesus who saves us is totally human. He is not pretending. He lived as we do, in questioning and anguish. It is very likely that the Agony in the Garden cost Jesus far more than the physical suffering of the crucifixion. And the better we understand the nature of Jesus' suffering, the better we will understand the impact of this scene.

Jesus refers to His suffering in the garden with the symbol of the cup. With complete honesty, He prays,

Abba, Father, ... take this cup away from me.
(Mk 14:36)

The symbol of the cup is used in two other places in the gospel to signify the death of Jesus. When James and John ask Jesus for the positions of privilege in His Kingdom, He responds,

You do not know what you are asking. Can you drink the cup that I drink or be baptized with the baptism with which I am baptized?
(Mk 10:38)

Here the cup refers to Jesus' sacrificial death as the symbol of the new covenant. The cup looks to the Cross. Drinking the cup is equivalent to sharing in Jesus' baptism by blood.

In the Last Supper account, there is also mention of the cup in reference to Jesus' death.

While they were eating, he took bread, said the blessing, broke it, and gave it to them, and said, "Take it; this is my body." Then he took a cup, gave thanks, and gave it to them, and they all drank from it. He said to them, "This is my blood of the covenant, which will be shed for many. Amen, I say to you, I shall not drink again the fruit of the vine until the day when I drink it new in the kingdom of God."

(Mk 14:22-25)

The cup contains the blood of Jesus poured out in His death on the Cross. Taking and drinking the cup of the new covenant, the disciples are joined to Christ in sacrifice on the Cross. Like James and John and all the apostles in the Upper Room, every follower of Jesus comes to share in the salvific effects of His Cross by receiving the sacraments of Baptism and the Eucharist and by living out these sacraments in life.

CHAPTER 7

THE LONELINESS OF THE CROSS

Then all the disciples left him and fled.

(Mt 26:56)

In the Agony in the Garden, it is hardly possible that Jesus is praying to the Father to remove the Cross from Him. At the Last Supper, He has already accepted His sacrificial death as redemptive for the sins of the world. Prior to this moment in Mark's gospel, Jesus has made three predictions of the Cross (Mk 8:31; 9:31; 10:33-34). In each of these sayings, there is an increasingly more vivid allusion to the physical pain of the crucifixion. In each prediction, Jesus expresses His unwavering acceptance of the Cross. No, it is not the bodily pain of crucifixion that tortures Jesus in Gethsemane. It is something else.

Mystery mingles with the night and darkens the interior struggle of Jesus in the garden. Yet, Mark gives us a hint to help us strain our feeble eyes to penetrate the clouds. Mark provides a way to understand some of the dense sorrow that closes in on Jesus right before His death.

Since Jesus in the Upper Room has already expressed His joyful willingness to die, the "cup" that He asks the Father to take away in His garden prayer means something other than His physical death on the Cross. "Cup" in biblical tradition is a symbol for punishment or pain (Is 51:17; Jer 25:15,17; Ps 75:9). By the way in which Mark frames his account of the Agony in the Garden, he indicates the nature of the pain which Jesus experiences.

As Jesus and the disciples make their way from the Upper Room to the Garden of Gethsemane, Jesus predicts the disciples' loss of faith. They all will desert Him when He is arrested. Quoting the prophet Zechariah 13:7, Jesus says:

> *All of you will have your faith shaken, for it is written: "I will strike the shepherd, and the sheep will be dispersed."* (Mk 14:27)

As Jesus leaves the garden, Mark indicates that Jesus' prediction is coming true. As the soldiers move in to arrest Him, Jesus cries out:

> *Have you come out as against a robber, with swords and clubs, to seize me? Day after day I was with you teaching in the temple area, yet you did not arrest me; but that the scriptures may be fulfilled.* (14:48-49)

And, then, Mark immediately tells us, *"And they all left him, and fled"* (14:50).

By beginning and ending the Agony in the Garden with reference to the prophecy of Zechariah, Mark is telling us that this Scripture passage explains the scene.

The actual passion is beginning. Jesus is moving from the Last Supper to the arrest to His trial and crucifixion. Jesus has gradually come to realize that His suffering and death will be a scandal to His disciples. The disciples will lose faith. He is the shepherd who will be struck. They are the sheep who will be scattered. In His death not only the body of Jesus will be broken, but also that small body of believers which He has carefully gathered around himself. What darkness must have crept into the heart of Jesus. He is to be alone in His suffering. His followers will abandon Him.

There are always certain things which we must settle in life in the silent solitude of our own soul. We may be very close to others and indeed find our strength multiplied by their love. Yet we make our great moral choices alone.

The eleven apostles accompany Jesus to the Mount of Olives. Peter, James, and John accompany Him to His place of prayer with the others left behind. These same three apostles had been with Him when He tenderly raised the daughter of Jairus to life (Mk 5:41). They had been with Him at the Transfiguration when they saw His earthly form radiate with the glory of heaven (Mk 9:2-8). They were close to Him when He gave His instructions on the last times (Mk 13:3). Now that those last times begin, they are with Him again, but not for long. They will fail to follow Him to the end. The rest of the journey Jesus will make alone. Now, in the Garden of Gethsemane, Jesus takes the first steps in that final journey by being alone with God in prayer, apart even from these favored three.

However, if the chief factor in Jesus' agony was His aloneness, Jesus would appear less than many martyrs who marched to their death without such intense turmoil. It was not simply the fact that His friends were deserting Him as much as the reality that these trusted friends were His followers. At this point in His life, they were the only visible token of His ministry. Now even these must be sacrificed. The last hope of success for His earthly ministry seems to be extinguished. Jesus recoils from the terrible realization that His suffering means the dissolution of the community of His followers. No one likes to die. But if in death, His life's work goes on, death is more bearable. Jesus is now facing the end of His life and His work on earth. And He is crushed. His offering will be complete.

CHAPTER 8

JESUS' PRAYER IN THE GARDEN

After withdrawing about a stone's throw from them and kneeling, he prayed... (Lk 22:41)

In his humanity, Jesus struggles to accept the Father's will in total abandonment. He takes His suffering to the Father in prayer in the Garden of Gethsemane. Jesus is a true son of Jacob who once spent the night wrestling with God before returning home to the Promised Land (Gen 32:22-32). Mark gives us insight into that nocturnal conversation that strengthened Jesus to accept His last sorrow.

The evangelist skillfully presents that garden prayer in three stages. First, Mark tells us,

He advanced a little and fell to the ground and prayed that if it were possible the hour might pass by him. (14:35)

Jesus is certainly willing to do the Father's will. Of this, there is no question. Yet, if God would will otherwise, Jesus could avoid the suffering of this hour. Mark's portrayal of Jesus is much more graphic than that in the gospel of Matthew or of Luke.

In the gospel of Matthew, Jesus falls on His face and prays (26:39). In Luke's gospel, He kneels down and prays (22:41). But, Mark tells us Jesus threw himself on the ground and prayed. Jesus appears less in control of himself in the gospel of Mark. And not only does He pray, but He prays over and over again. His anguished petition to the Father wells up from His sorrowing heart.

Next, Mark gives us the words of Jesus' prayer:

Abba, Father, all things are possible to you. Take this cup away from me, but not what I will but what you will. (14:36)

Jesus begins by addressing God as "Abba, Father." Mark preserves the original Aramaic form of address. In calling God "Abba," Jesus reveals His intense awareness of His own unique relationship to God. No Jew would ever dare address God as "Abba." The word was too familiar. It was the equivalent of our English word "Daddy."

In the gospels, only Jesus speaks to God so intimately. And, He does for the first time in this prayer. In that dark hour, Jesus speaks to God as the little child resting on His father's lap. He recognizes that, as troubling as His suffering was, He himself is not a victim of blind chance or the sport of cruel fate. God is His Father and He trusts He will never cause Him a useless tear.

In His prayer, Jesus is bringing our human nature in full obedience to the divine nature. He is proving himself to be the Son of the Father. God's will may mean mystery and even pain at times, but it is always love. In the garden, Jesus is the New Adam. Adam cowered in fear before God. Jesus rests confidently in His Father's embrace.

It is one thing in life to suffer for the wrong that we ourselves have done. In such a case, we resign ourselves to the difficulties in trying to right our wrongs. To straighten out the crooked is never easy. However, it is another thing to suffer for the good that we do. To put forth our best efforts and to have these fail is indeed more difficult. This is the pain of Jesus.

Jesus prays:

> *But not what I will but what you will.*
>
> (Mk 14:36)

Does Jesus cry those words in broken surrender? Certainly, for all of us, there are moments when we come up against insurmountable opposition and can do nothing but passively accept what cannot be otherwise. Or, does Jesus say that prayer with bitter resentment? We sometimes face moments in life when obstacles defeat our best efforts. Even though we accept our inability to change the situation, none-theless, we shake our fists in the face of fate. Neither! Jesus prays neither in helpless submission nor in hopeless surrender. Not at all!

Jesus prays in total love and complete trust. He is the Son trusting His Father. He not only accepts, but embraces His suffering. His prayer is actually His pledge of personal collaboration with the Father in the hours ahead. As Jesus faces His friends' failing

Him and His life falling apart, He entrusts himself wholly into the hands of His Father.

In his gospel, Luke records as the last prayer of the dying Jesus:

Father, into your hands I commit my spirit.

(23:46)

As Jesus leaves the world, He prays on the Cross as He prays in the Garden of Gethsemane. What He says so softly for the Father to hear in the garden in Mark's gospel, He cries out in a loud voice for all to hear on the Cross in Luke's gospel. His death truly is the sign of His divine Sonship. Jesus is one with the Father in will and in nature.

CHAPTER 9

THE COMPASSIONATE HIGH PRIEST

I pray for them. I do not pray for the world but for the ones you have given me. (Jn 17:9)

After Jesus' first prayer in the garden, He leaves His place of prayer and returns to Peter, James, and John. They are fast asleep. On his own, the evangelist would never have taken upon himself the liberty to speak of three of the Church's most important leaders in such a bad light. There must have been a genuine historical reminiscence behind his report. And, he is unashamed to report the weakness of the leaders. He knows that even the weakest of us can gain strength from the Savior. No matter what our personal failings are before the Lord, Jesus can still use anyone of His followers to lead others to himself. As Paul reminds us:

> *Consider your own calling, brothers. Not many of you were wise by human standards, not many were powerful, not many were of noble birth. Rather, God chose the foolish of the world to shame the wise, and God chose the weak of the world to shame the strong.*
>
> (1 Cor 1:26-27)

The sleep of the three apostles as Jesus prays in Gethsemane has cause for some endless problems.

How could the apostles have known what Jesus was praying if they were sound asleep? Did they simply put words on the lips of Jesus? Can we know for certain what Jesus actually said?

Careful attention to the prayer of Jesus in the garden provides the answer. Jesus' garden prayer reveals a startling similarity to the Our Father. First of all, in both prayers, God is addressed as "Father." Second, there is reference to doing the Father's will. And, third, there is reference to the final test or temptation. The disciples knew that, in giving them the Our Father, Jesus was giving them the very secret of His own intimate communion with the Father. His words in the garden, therefore, were not different from the way in which He always prayed nor from the way in which He commanded us to pray.

Upon returning to Peter, James, and John for the first time, the suffering Jesus speaks so sympathetically to His slumbering disciples. He tells them:

The spirit is willing, but the flesh is weak.

(Mk 14:38)

His words sound like some ancient proverb. Yet, neither biblical literature nor classical writings have produced it. No doubt in the heat of His own battle with disappointment, Jesus forged that maxim on the spot. In the deepest part of His soul, Jesus is willing to cooperate with the Father. Yet, His flesh, His human nature that He shares with us, is not at all eager to suffer.

What a noble individual Jesus truly is. He is grappling with the Father's will. He is entering the most intense suffering of His life on earth. Yet, He remains compassionate. He is not stern in rebuking His disciples for their weakness in falling asleep. He himself feels the same weakness as they do. As Hebrews tells us:

> *Every high priest is taken from among men and made their representative before God. . . . He is able to deal patiently with the ignorant and erring, for he himself is beset by weakness.*
>
> (5:1-2)

The compassion of Jesus at this point is a good lesson for us in dealing with others who let us down. Kindness, not cruelty, is the key to lasting friendship.

After speaking to His friends, Jesus returns to His prayer with the Father. Mark tells us:

> *And again he went away and prayed, saying the same words.* (14:39)

"The same words" refer to Jesus' saying "*the spirit is willing, but the flesh is weak*" (14:38). This time, however, He voices to God the very same words which He has just spoken to His sleeping disciples. In effect, He takes to the Father not simply His own situation but that of His friends as well. True communion with God alone in prayer draws us closer to those whom we love in life. We can never appear before God without bringing to our lips the needs of those we hold deep within our heart.

In this second prayer, Jesus is praying not for himself, but for others. This garden prayer of intercession resonates with the words of the Last Supper as recorded in the fourth gospel. Whether seated at table with His friends or kneeling with His Father, Jesus is always making intercession for us. As He himself says:

> *I pray for them. I do not pray for the world but for the ones you have given me, because they are yours....I pray not only for them, but also for those who will believe in me through their word, so that they may all be one, as you, Father, are in me and I in you, that they also may be in us, that the world may believe that you sent me.* (Jn 17:9, 20-21)

Jesus is the compassionate High Priest who truly understands our fallen human nature. He is one with us, able to sympathize with our weakness.

CHAPTER 10

THE GOOD SHEPHERD

I am the good shepherd. A good shepherd lays down his life for the sheep. (Jn 10:11)

After His second garden prayer, Jesus returns to His disciples and again discovers the disciples asleep. Though He speaks to them, they do not understand what He is saying nor do they know what to answer (Mk 14:40). Jesus leaves them and goes to pray a third time. With deliberate intent, Mark records the fact of Jesus' third prayer without giving the words which He uses. We are left wondering. What is Jesus thinking? Is His patience worn out? The suspense is ended when Jesus returns the third time and finds His disciples still asleep. He speaks to them for the last time:

Are you still sleeping and taking your rest? It is enough. (14:41)

Misunderstanding has now darkened to failure. Night has fallen. Yet Jesus is still loving to His own. He has repeatedly returned to these disciples, for He is the Good Shepherd who never abandons His lost sheep. He wants those who are with Him to be safe. And He is moved with great pity when they are lost (Mk 6:34). But now the Shepherd must be separated from His sheep. It is the moment for Jesus to begin the ascent to the Cross.

So He says:

> *The hour has come. Behold, the Son of Man is to be handed over to sinners. Get up, let us go. See, my betrayer is at hand.* (Mk 14:41b-42)

Jesus completely accepts the Father's will. It is His "hour," that is, the moment of His passing from this world to the Father. Even though His friends fail Him, He will remain faithful to His Father. Without reservation, He leaves behind what He has been called to surrender. Jesus' prayer has been effective. Three times He has prayed; and, He has been transformed. No longer does He lie prostrate with sorrow. He now stands up and goes forth to meet His enemies.

Jesus' threefold garden prayer is a lesson for us. By His own example, the Master is teaching us how to pray. We need never tire of bringing our petitions to God again and again. In prolonged dialogue with Him, we find the strength to do His will, we are changed. We become enabled by His grace to cooperate with His plan for our salvation.

Leaving the garden, Jesus walks toward the Cross. He had entered Gethsemane in the company of His disciples. He now exits alone. Mark has sandwiched this dramatic account of the Agony in the Garden between the Last Supper and the actual arrest. He has helped us see that the human Jesus who recoils from suffering is always the obedient Son who does the Father's will. Jesus is truly the compassionate Shepherd who cares for His lost sheep, even if He must suffer and die alone. In the Garden of Eden, surrounded by the pleasures of this world, one man sinned and we all fell from grace. In the Garden of Gethsemane, one man, stripped of all worldly consolation and prostrate with sorrow stood up and all of us rose to new life.

They brought him to the place of Golgotha (which is translated Place of the Skull). They gave him wine drugged with myrrh, but he did not take it. Then they crucified him..."

(Mk 15:22-24)

CHAPTER 11

THE CRUCIFIED SAVIOR

Jesus the Nazorean was a man commended to you by God with mighty deeds, wonders, and signs…. This man, delivered up by the set plan and foreknowledge of God, you killed using lawless men to crucify him. (Acts 2:22-23)

At the center of the Passion narrative is the crucifixion. Originally, crucifixion was a punishment reserved by the Romans for slaves. So abhorrent was death by crucifixion that Cicero said that *"the very name 'cross' should be far from the body of a Roman citizen, but also from his thoughts, his eyes and his ears."* He labelled it the *"most cruel and disgusting penalty."*

Fixed to the cross, the condemned would suffer excruciating physical pain and emotional distress. The agony could go on for days. Often, the Romans would leave the corrupting bodies on their crosses as a grim deterrent to would-be offenders of Roman law.

In the time of Jesus, the Romans crucified not only slaves, but any criminal convicted of treason, rebellion, piracy, sedition, or robbery. During the siege of Jerusalem in 70 A.D., the Romans crucified their Jewish prisoners, nailing them in different positions to their crosses to increase their pain. In this way,

according to Josephus, the Jewish historian, "the soldiers, out of rage and hatred, amused themselves."
The Romans would crucify as many as five hundred
captives in a single day. So hardened their hearts!

The Romans chose Golgotha as the place to crucify Jesus (Mk 15:22–25; Mt 27:33–35; Jn 19:17–24).
It was located just outside the city walls near the
well-travelled Jerusalem Jaffa Road. In this way, the
dying Jesus could be seen and serve as a warning to
many. The soldiers fasten Jesus to the Cross. He is
just another victim of Roman justice. His crucifixion
is mere routine for them. But not for the evangelists.

All four evangelists simply say, *"they crucified
him"* (Mk 15:24; Mt 27:35; Lk 23:33; Jn 19:18). So
painful, so inhumane, so cruel, so ignominious was
death by crucifixion that not a single gospel writer
can bring himself to detail the gruesome acts of
nailing the hands and feet of Jesus to the wooden
crossbeam and then hoisting it up on the stake in the
ground. They shield our eyes from the horror. Jesus
ascends Golgotha one moment; and the next, He
hangs helpless and unresisting on the Cross, mocked
and scorned.

In the Passion narrative, there is a recurrence
of threes. Peter denies Jesus three times. Jesus
offers three petitions in His prayer in the Garden of
Gethsemane; and, three times, He finds His disciples
fast asleep. As He suffers His final hours nailed to the
Cross, three groups of people mock and revile Him.

The first group to hurl their insults at the Cross are the casual passers-by.

> *Those passing by blasphemed him, shaking their heads and saying, "Aha! You who would destroy the temple and rebuild it in three days, save yourself by coming down from the cross."*
> (Mk 15:29-30)

These individuals either do not know Jesus or have remained unimpressed by His miracles. Seeing Jesus stripped of all earthly power, they contemptuously hurl at Him His own claim that He would destroy the Temple and raise it up in three days. They repeat the very claim made against Him in His trial before the chief priests and elders (Mk 15:28). How ironic that what they judge by human standards that Jesus could not do, He is accomplishing before their eyes. By dying on the Cross, He is replacing the Temple in Jerusalem with the new Temple, His Resurrected Body. Now *"true worshippers will worship the Father in Spirit and truth"* (Jn 4:23).

Seeing Him punished in company with the two malefactors, one on His right and one on His left, those who pass by presume that Jesus is as guilty as the others. Presumption is always the stepchild of pride. The proud always falsely judge others. They cannot identify with those who suffer. *"Enough of good there is in the lowest estate to sweeten life; enough of evil in the highest to check presumption; enough there is of both in all estates, to bind us in*

*compassionate brotherhood, to teach us impressively
that we are of one dying and one immortal family"*
(Henry Giles).

The passers-by who mock Jesus do not have even
the kindness to stand still at the sight of suffering.
As they pass by on their way to attend to their own
mundane interests, they wag their heads and scoff at
Jesus. In the Old Testament, this is how the wicked
taunt the just man.

> *All who see me mock me; they curl their lips
> and jeer; they shake their heads at me.*
>
> (Ps 22:8)

Thus, for both Mark and Matthew, these individuals who casually take notice of the suffering Jesus
and mock Him are truly wicked. No sympathy touch-
es their hearts. Jesus, however, is the Just One.

At the beginning of His public ministry, Jesus'
enemies had accused Him of blasphemy because He
forgave sin. No man can forgive sins. Only God can
forgive sins. At the end of His life, the Sanhedrin
also condemned Him for blasphemy. They rightly
understood that Jesus claimed not simply to be the
Messiah, but to be God (Mk 14:61-64; Mt 26:63-66).
Blasphemy is a sin only against God. By telling us
that the passers-by "blaspheme" Jesus, Mark is telling us that Jesus is truly divine. In the mystery of
the Cross, His humanity is broken and His divinity is
revealed. God is love and love suffers all.

The chief priests, the scribes, and the elders make up the second group to deride Jesus on the Cross. These men represent the highest religious authority of the Jewish people. In their fierce hostility, they now oppose the highest authority.

> *Likewise the chief priests with the scribes and elders mocked him and said, "He saved others; he cannot save himself. So he is the king of Israel! Let him come down from the cross now, and we will believe in him. He trusted in God; let him deliver him now if he wants him. For he said, 'I am the Son of God.'"*

(Mt 27:41-43)

In Jesus' trial before Pilate, some of the religious leaders of the Jews had manipulated the rabble to have the guilty Barabbas released and the innocent Jesus crucified. At the Cross, they join in mockery of the mob, whom they despised. Seeing Jesus suffer, they "sneer" at Him (Lk 23:35). The smirk on their faces reveals their pleasure that Jesus is being put to death. He will be gone from their midst. Their position will be secure. How little do they know! His very death and resurrection is ushering in the new dispensation of grace. In a short time, they will be gone and their Temple destroyed by the Romans.

Ever intent on their self-importance, these religious leaders position themselves apart from the crowd. The passers-by had spoken directly to Jesus, taunting Him. But these supercilious religious stand at a distance. They speak among themselves, loud enough for all to hear. They attack Him with their barbed sarcasm, saying that He who saved others cannot save His own life.

During His public ministry, Jesus had indeed saved others. He saved the lepers from being cast out, the blind from their prison of darkness, and the possessed from the chains of Satan. He even saved some from the jaws of death. He raised up the daughter of Jairus, the son of the widow of Nain, and the brother of Martha and Mary, His own beloved friend Lazarus. They are right. He did save others. But, they were wrong, saying that He cannot save himself.

Jesus never used His divine power for His own advantage. And, He does not use it to come down from the Cross. What proves that He is truly the Son of God is precisely His remaining on the Cross and loving us, even to the point of death. As Son, He *"humbled himself, becoming obedient to death, even death on a cross"* (Phil 2:8). Jesus did not come down from the Cross. He stayed there and lifted us up. Unbelievers will always demand miracles. But, the greatest miracle is the love of God who dies for sinners. Unlike the teachers of this world, Jesus attracts us to be His disciples not so much by His words, but by love. And so, true discipleship, following Jesus, is always a love affair!

The third group to mock Jesus on the Cross are the two criminals crucified on either side of Him.

Those who were crucified with him also kept abusing him. (Mk 15:32)

These men are revolutionaries. They had rebelled against Rome. They are being punished for their crimes of sedition and robbery. They are sinners. They have transgressed the law and are paying the price. Dying in their company, Jesus is fulfilling the prophecy of Isaiah: *"he surrendered himself to death, was counted among the transgressors, bore the sins of many, and interceded for the transgressors"* (Is 53:12).

As the Suffering Servant of Isaiah, Jesus *"bore the sins of many."* The word "many" is a Semitic expression that means "the totality" or "all." The scapegoat sent into the desert on the Day of Atonement bore the sins of one nation alone. Jesus, the Lamb of God, takes away the sins of the entire world. Jesus' sacrifice on the Cross is our constant forgiveness for our daily sins and our steadfast strength in our struggles. It is His priestly intercession that makes us holy.

Seeing Jesus, the Suffering Servant, silently, nobly bearing His suffering, intensifies the anger of those crucified with Him. They turn their venom on Jesus by reviling Him in the very same way that the others do (Mt 27:44). The first two gospels record their cruelty in the single sentence: *"they abused him."* Mark says that *"they kept abusing him."* The imperfect of the verb indicates that their derision is continuous.

Luke does more than simply mention the mockery of those crucified with Jesus. He details their taunts. The criminal on the left derides Jesus with the very same insults as the Roman soldiers did. And, he repeats the same scoffs that the Jewish authorities had hurled against their victim. His words come as the culmination of the hatred that surrounds the dying Jesus.

However, the innocence of Jesus moves the criminal to the right of Jesus to feel pity for Him. Seeing Jesus' goodness, he "rebukes" the other wrongdoer for his insolence. Even in the worst of circumstances, goodness can be found. Rebuking him, he said,

> *Have you no fear of God.... we have been condemned justly.* (Lk 23:40-41)

As Jesus rebuked Satan three times in the desert (Lk 4:35, 39, 41), this man recognizes evil in his fellow criminal and "rebukes" him. We should *"never be afraid to do what is right, especially if the well-being of a person is at stake....Society's punishments are small compared to the wound we inflict on our souls when we look the other way"* (Martin Luther King).

Not looking the other way, the criminal to the right turns from condemning evil to asking for forgiveness. He is the single individual to speak to Jesus on the Cross without mocking His claims to be the Messiah or taunting Him with jeers and blasphemies. He is the single individual to offer Him the homage of a kind word. With the eyes of faith, he sees beyond the tortured body of Jesus purpled in blood and acknowledges Jesus' royal dignity. He pleads:

Jesus, remember me when you come into your kingdom. (Lk 23:42)

This repentant wrongdoer, whom tradition has baptized the good thief, is the last person to speak to Jesus before Jesus dies. He calls on Jesus simply, confidently, by His name alone. Nowhere in the entire gospel tradition does anyone ever address Jesus so tenderly, so intimately. In every other place, the name Jesus is qualified. But not here. And, his words elicit from Jesus the assurance of forgiveness:

Amen, I say to you, today you will be with me in Paradise. (Lk 23:43)

Instantly that divine absolution turns a sinner into a saint and opens for him the gates of heaven. It is never too late to receive the mercy of Christ. No sin, too great. No moment, too late. *"Everyone who calls on the name of the Lord will be saved"* (Rom 10:13).

*You were ransomed...not with perish-
able things like silver or gold but with
the precious blood of Christ as of a
spotless unblemished lamb...known
before the foundation of the world but
revealed in the final time for you.*
(1 Pt 1:18-20)

CHAPTER 12

THE LAMB OF GOD

Behold, the Lamb of God, who takes away the sin of the world. (Jn 1:29)

The traveler who has reached the highest attainable summit of the Andes and stands in the pure, cloudless air can enjoy an almost boundless horizon. But whoever remains in the valley below amidst the haze and vapor must be satisfied with a lesser view. Much of the surrounding beauty escapes notice. So it is with all of us as we travel through this life. Dimness obscures the divine mercy and richness of God's love that surrounds us.

Yet, there is a way by which the Christian can gain a wider perspective. There is an elevation which we can climb that commands the boundless extent of God's love. It is Golgotha.

In Aramaic, "Golgotha" means skull. Legend has it that it was the burial ground of Adam. This is why artists often depict a skull at the foot of the Cross. On this spot, the new Adam rose above the first Adam. With the fourth evangelist as our guide, we can ascend that hill and, once our feet are firmly set upon its summit, we can let our eyes stretch to take in the view.

John helps us see what takes place on Calvary in three ways. He fixes our eyes on what is happening before us. He then stretches our gaze backward to past events that have led up to this moment. And finally, he invites us to peer into the future that will unfold in the world because of the Cross.

With John, we see Jesus dragging His cross up the hill. Unlike the other evangelists, John omits mentioning Simon of Cyrene who assists Jesus in carrying the Cross (Mk 15:21; Mt 27:32; Lk 23:26). John would have us take no notice of Simon. He wants us to realize that Jesus is in control of His own suffering and death. Jesus goes alone to the Cross. It is His choice. Remember Jesus' own words during His public ministry:

> *This is why the Father loves me, because I lay down my life in order to take it up again. No one takes it from me, but I lay it down on my own. I have power to lay it down, and power to take it up again. This command I have received from my Father.* (Jn 10:17-18)

Willingly and not by force, the Good Shepherd sacrifices His life for His sheep.

After fixing our eyes on Jesus on His way to the Cross, with the swiftness of an eagle, John peers into the past and makes our glance travel across the many ups and downs of Israel's history to another hill. It is Mt. Moriah. There Isaac is carrying the wood for sacrifice (Gen 22:6). There Abraham, with heavy steps, marks out each pace to the moment of sacrifice.

When his young and only son Isaac innocently questions his father, *"Where is the sheep for a burnt offering"* (Gen 22:7), the patriarch becomes prophet. Abraham replies, *"My son...God will provide himself the sheep for the burnt offering"* (Gen 22:8). In the actual events on Mt. Moriah, it was not a lamb, but a ram caught in the bushes that Abraham sacrificed to God in place of his own son. It is on Calvary that Abraham's prophecy finds fulfillment. For God who did spare Isaac did not spare His only-begotten Son. He allowed Jesus to die on the Cross. John makes us remember this event by telling us that, at the very hour when the paschal lambs were being slaughtered in the temple, Jesus dies (Jn 19:14). Jesus is the lamb which God provides for our redemption. Jesus, indeed, is both the Good Shepherd who lays down His life and the pure lamb led to slaughter. Priest and victim are one in the perfect sacrifice of the Cross.

Finally, John makes our eyes race into the future. The soldier is thrusting his sharp sword into the side of Jesus *"and immediately blood and water flowed out"* (19:34). The blood proves that the lamb has been truly sacrificed. But, there is more. Jesus' blood poured out for us from the Cross is His blood poured out for us in the Eucharist. Jesus, the Lamb of God, has become our food and drink in the Eucharist (Jn 6:51-58). In receiving Him, the true paschal lamb, we pass over from the slavery of sin to the newness of grace, from death to life.

The water that flows from Jesus' pierced side symbolizes the gift of the Holy Spirit (Jn 7:37-39) who gives new life to us in Baptism (Jn 3:5-6). In the old creation, four rivers in the Garden of Eden ran towards the ends of the earth, giving life and bringing fruitfulness in their path (Gen 2:10-14). Now, in the new creation, there flows from the pierced side of Jesus the grace of redemption sweeping sin away and bearing the believer to Paradise.

Chapter 13

MARY AT THE CROSS

Standing by the cross of Jesus were his mother, his mother's sister, Mary the wife of Clopas, and Mary of Magdala. (Jn 19:25)

As we stand with John the Beloved Disciple on Golgotha, the evangelist shows us seven scenes from the moment that Jesus ascends the summit of that hill until the moment He is taken down from the Cross and buried. These seven tableaux are: the crucifixion (19:16-18); placing of the inscription on the Cross (19:19-22); dividing Jesus' garments (19:23-24); Jesus' entrusting His mother to the beloved disciple (19:25-27); the death of Jesus (19:28-30); the piercing of Jesus' side (19:31-37); the burial (19:38-42). In each event, the evangelist sees the present, remembers the past, and peers into the future.

At the very center of these seven scenes stands Mary at the foot of the Cross. Three scenes precede it; three follow it. And, so in looking at this one picture, we are coming to the heart of the crucifixion event.

The evangelist contemplates a dying son caring for His mother, His most precious worldly treasure. Since the Blessed Virgin Mary had no other children, her only son entrusts her to His cousin, John. The gift enriches both and holds for all a needed lesson.

Suffering the horrors of the crucifixion, Jesus looks beyond His own pain to the tears of His widowed mother and provides for her well-being. During His ministry, Jesus had raised from the dead the only son of the widow of Nain. He did this miracle unsolicited. Pure compassion moved His heart. And, this is the very same compassion that He, the only son, shows to His own widowed mother as He dies on the Cross.

In so doing, He has set for us a powerful example. Those who follow Him can never claim personal inconvenience as a reason for neglecting their parents, especially when they are aged and infirm. Jesus once said He did not come to abolish, but to fulfill the law. He went on to pronounce blessed anyone who observes even the smallest details of the law (Mt 5:17-20). And so as He dies in obedience to the law of nature, He fulfills the divine law of the fourth commandment to honor one's parents.

In this scene of Mary at the foot of the Cross, the fourth evangelist sees more than a son tenderly caring for His mother. The event is freighted with meaning. Deliberately John refers to Mary not by her personal name, but by the title "woman." She stands there not only as the mother of a condemned man, but also as something more. Mary appears in John's gospel at Cana and at Calvary. Both times, the evangelist does not use her name. Instead, he uses the title "woman." This way of referring to Mary reveals her role in the drama of salvation.

When the evangelist speaks of Mary as "woman" at the Cross, this title triggers a flashback for the evangelist. John is remembering what Jesus said at the Last Supper. Then, too, Jesus spoke of a woman:

Amen, amen, I say to you, you will weep and mourn, while the world rejoices; you will grieve, but your grief will become joy. When a woman is in labor, she is in anguish because her hour has arrived; but when she has given birth to a child, she no longer remembers the pain because of her joy that a child has been born into the world. So you also are now in anguish. But I will see you again, and your hearts will rejoice, and no one will take your joy away from you. (16:20-22)

Here, with the image of "the woman in labor," Jesus is alluding to two passages from the prophet Isaiah in order to speak about His own disciples who witness His passion and death.

In the first passage, a prayer of God's people for the final age, for Isaiah says:

As a woman about to give birth writhes and cries out in pain, so were we before you, Lord.
(Is 26:17)

In the second passage, an oracle of salvation, the prophet Isaiah uses the image of the woman about to give birth to speak of Zion, the Chosen People who give birth to the Messiah.

Before she is in labor,
she gives birth; before her pangs come upon
  her, she delivers a male child.
Who ever heard of such a thing,
or who ever saw the like?
Can a land be brought forth in one day,
or a nation be born in a single moment?
Yet Zion was scarcely in labor
when she bore her children.
Shall I bring a mother to the point of birth, and
  yet not let her child be born? says the Lord.
Or shall I who bring to birth
yet close her womb? says your God.
Rejoice with Jerusalem and be glad because
  of her, all you who love her;
Rejoice with her in her joy,
all you who mourn over her.

(Is 66:7-10)

According to Isaiah, the Messianic age when God establishes His reign on earth will be a new birth for the world. And, since the Messiah will come from the womb of Israel, all the faithful will suffer the birth pangs of the new age.

At the Last Supper, Jesus sees these prophecies of Isaiah fulfilled in himself. His death and Resurrection are a new birth for the world. And, His disciples are the New Israel. Jesus has been among them like the fertile seed in the womb. As He passes from death to life, they are the woman in labor, for the Messiah is being born to new life from their midst. Certainly they sorrow now in the birth pangs of Calvary. But soon they will forget that suffering in the overwhelming joy of the Resurrection.

In the last book of the New Testament, John also makes use of this image of the woman in labor.

A great sign appeared in the sky, a woman clothed with the sun, with the moon under her feet, and on her head a crown of twelve stars. She was with child and wailed aloud in pain as she labored to give birth. (Rev 12:1-2)

In this passage, the woman is an ambivalent figure. On the one hand, she stands for the faithful remnant on earth, the faithful who suffer for their faith and persevere. The woman, therefore, represents the Church under persecution.

On the other hand, the woman symbolizes the Church in a state of glory. As the bride in the Song of Songs, she is pictured *"fair as the moon, bright as the sun"* (Sg 6:10). She is clothed with all possible light because she is the Bride of Christ in the fullness of perfection (Eph 5:25-27). She is crowned with twelve stars, representing the twelve tribes of Israel and the twelve apostles.

The woman stands with the moon beneath her feet. As the sun reigns by day, the moon rules by night, overcoming the darkness. Thus, the woman treading on the moon is pictured as conquering the forces of evil. In this image of the woman, there flashes before our eyes royalty, authority, and victory. Even though the Church appears small among the kingdoms of the world and persecuted, she is, nonetheless, the Royal Lady clothed with the fullness of heavenly glory and triumphant.

The fourth evangelist uses the title "woman" against this background. In the sorrowful scene at Calvary, Mary represents the believers who remain faithful to Jesus despite persecution. She also symbolizes in her person Mother Zion, the Church, who brings forth new children and triumphs over evil.

Chapter 14

MARY THE MOST FAITHFUL DISCIPLE

Blessed is she who has believed... (Lk 1:45)

Of all those disciples who have been with Jesus, of all those who have been faithful, Mary is herself the first and most faithful disciple. At the Annunciation, the angel Gabriel announces to Mary that she is to be the mother of Jesus, who is the Messiah, the Son of David and the Son of God. In Luke's gospel, this is the first proclamation of the gospel; and, Mary who accepts and believes that word is the very first Christian disciple (Lk 1:26-38).

When the angel Gabriel announces to the aged Zachary the birth of John the Baptist, Zachary doubts the angel's message and is struck dumb. When Gabriel announces to Mary the birth of Jesus, Mary shows no hesitancy, no reluctance to believe. She utters her fiat of total obedience to God's will. God is all-powerful and His omnipotence makes fertile even her physical barrenness. Mary is a virgin. And it is her virginal trust in the Lord that is the rich soil receptive for the Word of God whom she embraces in faith. As St. Augustine says, the Virgin *"conceived in her heart before her womb"* (*Discourses*, 215, 4). She conceived first faith and then the Lord.

Mary is also the most faithful. She never abandons Jesus, not even in His public ministry. From Cana to Calvary, she accompanies her son.

More than any other she is the woman who suffers the birth pains of the new age. She is "the woman" for the fourth evangelist as she stands at the foot of the Cross. All around her can be heard the blasphemy of the godless, the scoffing of the sinner, the taunt of the impious. Yet Mary, "the woman," stands in silence. The sun itself hides its face. Nature herself quivers as humankind kills its God. Yet Mary stands firm and courageous. It is a solemn posture appropriate for someone offering sacrifice. In those moments, Mary joins with Jesus as He offers to the Father the Body and Blood He received from her spotless womb.

The others had once watched with Mary when Jesus turned water into wine that bright, sunny day in Cana. They had witnessed the feeding of the five thousand, the cure of the nobleman's son, and many other miracles besides. With open mouths, they had even witnessed Jesus raise Lazarus from the tomb. But now that wonders ceased, their faith fails.

How easy it is for all of us to believe in a loving God when the sun smiles joyfully on our life. But let a rain cloud pass by and immediately the warmth of our faith begins to chill. True faith never forgets. And that was the faith that brought Mary to the Cross.

Mary never rested her faith in what Jesus did. Long before He had worked a single miracle, she already believed in Him. She was the one who noticed the embarrassing situation of the wine running out at Cana and had enough trust in her son merely to state, *"They have no wine"* (Jn 2:3). With utter confidence in His concern for others and His power, she then said to the waiter-in-charge, *"Do whatever he tells you"* (Jn 2:5). Now when all signs have ceased, Mary stays with her son, ready to do whatever He says. Like the ivy that clings to the castle in summer's heat and winter's blasting, she holds on to Jesus in faith and in love.

Faith in her son made her strong enough to break the barriers of ridicule and hatred and stay by His side. Faith is strength, especially when it is supported by love. In Mary "the woman," we see present two of the strongest powers at work in the world—faith and love. If these two are at odds, the struggle is immense. If they are one, even the weakest becomes unshaken.

With faith, we can surrender what we hold most dear to our hearts, including those persons whose love we treasure most. For when we give to God what belongs to Him, we receive back our gift in the way most suited to our needs.

Standing by the cross of Jesus were his mother and his mother's sister, Mary the wife of Clopas, and Mary of Magdala. (Jn 19:25)

Chapter 15

MARY OUR MOTHER

Behold, your mother! (Jn 19:27)

When Jesus looked down from the Cross, He saw His faithful mother and the disciple whom He loved. As Nicodemus is the symbol of all the learned who seek after the truth (Jn 3:1-21) and the Samaritan woman, the symbol of the unsophisticated looking for the living water (Jn 4:4-42), the beloved disciple at the foot of the Cross represents every follower who loves the Master. Throughout the fourth gospel, he is the ideal disciple. He never deserts Jesus. He is particularly sensitive to Jesus, resting his head against Jesus at the Last Supper (Jn 13:23). After the Resurrection, he is the first of the Twelve to come to faith (Jn 20:3-8). In the person of John, therefore, are present all who believe in Jesus.

Looking down at both Mary and the beloved disciple, Jesus speaks two words of revelation:

When Jesus saw his mother and the disciple whom he loved standing near, he said to his mother, "Woman, Behold your son!" Then he said to the disciple, "Behold your mother!" And from that hour the disciple took her to his home. (Jn 19:26-27)

79

Jesus is proclaiming a new motherhood and a new sonship from the pulpit of the Cross. They belong to God's plan for the salvation of the world.

This is the last time Jesus ever speaks to Mary. He tells her that she is to have other children: the beloved disciple and all whom He represents. An angel had made the first Annunciation, God's Son makes the second. The silent solitude of the Annunciation gives way to a crowd of onlookers; the secluded garden to the mountain-top. The Church is being born in the birth pangs of the Cross; and, Mary is her Mother.

On Calvary, Jesus is establishing a new family. He had hinted at this during His ministry. All the Synoptic gospels report that six months after Jesus had settled His headquarters in Capernaum, a family delegation paid Him a visit (Mk 3:31-35; Mt 12:46-50; Lk 8:19-21). Jesus was inside the house. A crowd was attentively listening to His word. Since His family could not enter the crowded house, they sent Jesus the word *"your mother and brothers are standing outside and want to see you"* (Lk 8:20). According to the gospels of Matthew and Mark, Jesus responds with the question *"Who are my mother and my brothers?"* (Mk 3:33; see Mt 12:48). He, then, points to those disciples seated around Him and says:

> *Here are my mother and my brothers. Whoever does the will of God is my brother and sister and mother.* (Mk 3:34-35; see Mt 12:49-50)

At first glance, it may seem as if Jesus is making a pointed comparison between His family on the outside and his new family on the inside. Those on the outside are His physical family. They share the same generation of flesh and blood. Those on the inside are His spiritual family. They share in the same regeneration that comes from God.

Certainly, Jesus is dramatically stating that belonging to His new family means more than having the same bonds of the flesh. But, in no way is He excluding Mary from this new family. He is merely defining what constitutes membership. Luke makes this clear. In his gospel, when Jesus hears His mother and brothers are on the outside, He says:

> *My mother and my brothers are those who hear the word of God and act on it.* (8:21)

For Luke, Mary who stands outside the house is truly inside the new family which Jesus is forming by His life, death, and Resurrection.

At the very beginning of his gospel, Luke gives us Mary's first response to God:

> *Behold, I am the handmaid of the Lord; may it be done to me according to your word.*
>
> (1:38)

Mary receives God's word and obeys it. In the scene of Mary and Jesus' family on the outside and Jesus on the inside teaching His followers, Luke is telling us that Mary is one who continually hears the word of God and does it. This is the only time Luke brings together Mary and the brothers of Jesus; and, he does so in terms of obedience to God's word as faithful disciples of Jesus and members of God's new family. Already Luke is anticipating within the ministry of Jesus the picture of the Church he will paint on the opening pages of Acts.

In the first chapter of Acts of the Apostles, we see the Church filled with the Holy Spirit. It is exactly as we see it here: Mary together with the believing disciples (Acts 1:14). This is the ideal Christian community. And, John the fourth evangelist places it first at the foot of the Cross.

Believing in Jesus brings Mary and the beloved disciple to the Cross and believing in Christ Crucified joins us to them. For us, as for them, it means holding on to Jesus not only in bright days when He works great wonders in our life but in dark days when He hangs helpless on a Cross.

Holding on to Jesus sooner or later will mean letting go of prized possessions. It is only in emptying ourselves of the obstacles to God's love that we can become more open to the gift of divine life. The ocean flows inland and takes the shape imposed upon the contours of the banks. So too, the love of God when poured out into our hearts rushes in where we have emptied ourselves of our own desires.

Mary and the beloved disciple stand at the Cross, emptied of the hopes that they had cherished for Jesus' ushering in the kingdom of God. Jesus gives them the gift of the Holy Spirit, filling them with His divine life, and making them mother and son in a new, spiritual sense.

The moment and the gift are of supreme significance for salvation, for John indicates that, after this, Jesus knew that everything had been completed (19:28). Indeed, Jesus has finished the work the Father gave Him to do. He has formed the family of God.

In the prologue of his gospel, the fourth evangelist had said of Jesus:

He came to what was his own, but his own people did not accept him. But to those who did accept him he gave power to become children of God, to those who believe in his name, who were born not by natural generation nor by human choice nor by a man's decision but of God. (1:11-13)

Thus, at the beginning of his gospel, John had told us that Jesus came to form a new family and make us all children of God. As Jesus dies, He is triumphant, for, at the Cross, that new family is born with Mary as our Mother.

In the beginning was the Word, and the Word was with God, and the Word was God. *(Jn 1:1)*

CHAPTER 16

THE MYSTERY REVEALED

Truly this man was the Son of God! (Mk 15:39)

In God's plan, it is the Cross that fully reveals the mystery of Jesus. Before the Passion, a silence surrounds the mystery of Jesus. When the demons recognize who Jesus is, they are forbidden to make Jesus known (Mk 1:34; 3:12). When the disciples begin to understand something of the mystery of Jesus, they are told not to reveal Jesus' true identity (Mk 8:30; 9:9). Those healed are prohibited from publishing the miracles in order to keep Jesus' identity a secret (Mk 1:43; 5:43; 7:36). But in the Passion, that silence is shattered. At first this is done symbolically; then it is done with solemn statement.

On Wednesday of the last week of Jesus' life, Jesus is dining in the home of Simon, the leper. A woman enters the house and, in an unforgettable gesture of love, anoints Jesus. She breaks open a jar of pure nard worth about a year's wages and lavishly pours it over Jesus. To some, this extravagance seemed a waste. The selfish can never understand love, for love always gives spontaneously without counting the costs.

Whereas the fourth evangelist tells us the woman anointed Jesus' feet (Jn 12:3), Mark indicates she poured the oil over Jesus' head (Mk 14:3). For Mark, this is a royal gesture. Kings were anointed on the head and Jesus is now about to be crowned as king in the events of His suffering, death, and resurrection. Interesting enough, this account of the woman anointing Jesus on the head is sandwiched between the conspiracy of the chief priests and scribes to kill Jesus (Mk 14:1-2) and the betrayal of Judas (Mk 14:10-11). It is a woman who stands out as a symbol of love in the midst of man's great hostility.

At the center of the Passover narrative comes the most solemn statement of Jesus about His kingdom. What this woman's deed only whispers in symbol, Jesus himself proclaims in words. With great artistic skill, the evangelist relates this moment.

Jesus stands erect in the house of the high priest, while, at the same time, Peter is stooped over the fire in the courtyard. Peter shudders in the brisk night air as he moves farther and farther away from Jesus. A servant-girl recognizes the Prince of the Apostles. She confronts him, saying:

You too were with the Nazarene, Jesus.

(Mk 14:67)

He denies it and tries to get away from her. She follows him and points him out to those standing around. Peter becomes angry and denies once again his association with Jesus. Finally, the bystanders themselves interrogate him:

Surely you are one of them; for you too are a Galilean. (Mk 14:70)

In response, Peter vehemently disavows that he even knew Jesus.

He began to invoke a curse on himself and to swear, "I do not know this man of whom you speak." (Mk 14:71)

Peter has not only denied the truth, but his lying has led him to profanation and to total separation from his Master. The Rock of the Church is crushed. Like so many other sinners, Peter, having fallen once, sins more easily a second and a third time. For once we are on the decline, gravity and time determine how low we go. Peter had once scaled the heights of faith's confession at Caesarea Philippi (Mk 8:27-30); now he sinks to the depths of denial. All of us are indeed capable of being friend or foe to Jesus. We bear the responsibility to only one title for eternity.

Strangely enough, as Jesus' own prophecy of Peter's denial is coming true outside the house, inside Jesus is being mocked as a prophet:

Some began to spit on him, and to cover his face, and to strike him, saying to him, "Prophesy!" (Mk 14:65)

Peter is loudly protesting before his examiners. Jesus is deliberately silent before His accusers. He maintains an eloquent silence only to be broken at the proper moment.

When His enemies find not a single piece of evidence that would condemn Him, in utter desperation, the high priest asks Jesus directly:

Are you the Messiah, the Son of the Blessed One. (Mk 14:61)

Unknowingly, the high priest is using the same title that Peter had given Jesus at Caesarea Philippi when he acknowledged Jesus as "the Messiah," that is, "the Christ" (Mk 8:29). The high priest then adds the second title "the Son of the Blessed One" (Mk 14:61). This title is another way of saying "Son of God."

In the opening verse of his gospel, Mark includes the very same titles for Jesus that are found on the lips of the high priest:

The beginning of the gospel of Jesus Christ, the Son of God. (1:1)

The first half of his gospel climaxes with the title "the Christ" or "the Messiah" spoken by Peter at Caesarea Philippi. The second half of the Gospel concludes with the title "the Son of God" uttered by the centurion at the foot of the Cross. As Mark relates:

When the centurion who stood facing him saw how he breathed his last he said, "Truly this man was the Son of God!" (15:39)

By placing both titles "Christ" (Messiah) and Son of "the Blessed One" (God) on the lips of the high priest just as Jesus is about to be handed over to be crucified, the evangelist is saying that Jesus' suffering and death reveal His full identity that has been kept hidden during His public ministry.

Finally, in response to the high priest's interrogation, the Incarnate Word breaks His silence. He not only claims to be the Messiah but also reveals His divinity (Mk 14:62). Once Jesus affirms His equality with the Father, Jesus is condemned to death for blasphemy. By confessing the truth, Jesus is leading the procession of Christians who refuse to deny or compromise the faith. Truth is never to be compromised despite the personal suffering.

About three that afternoon, the night hastening from her chamber, suddenly usurps the day. Nature hides her face in shame as a hushed silence falls on the bystanders. Jesus unexpectedly cries out with a loud voice (Mk 15:34, 37).

Twice outside the Passion narrative, the evangelist uses this expression "with a loud voice." In the synagogue of Capernaum, the unclean spirit throws a man into convulsions and, then, comes out of him *"with a loud cry"* (Mk 1:26). When the Gadarene demoniac catches sight of Jesus at a distance, he runs up to Jesus, falls at His feet, and cries out *"with a loud voice"* (Mk 5:7). In each instance, it is someone oppressed by evil who cries out in a loud voice.

On the Cross, the evil of the world presses in on Jesus. He feels alone and abandoned. And so He cries out with a loud voice:

*Eloi, Eloi, lema sabachthani? which is trans-
lated, My God, my God, why have you forsak-
en me?* (Mk l5:34)

Jesus' prayer pierces the darkness of Calvary. He
is reciting the opening words of Psalm 22, a psalm
that begins on a note of despair but ends with great
trust. The simple fact that Jesus even prays means
He is not despairing. In Hebrew piety, to cite the first
words of a psalm meant praying the entire psalm.
This particular psalm ends on a note of total trust in
the Father:

*For he has not spurned or disdained
the misery of this poor wretch,
Did not turn away from me,
but heard me when I cried out.
I will offer praise in the great assembly; my
     vows I will fulfill before those who fear him…
All the ends of the earth
will remember and turn to the Lord
All the families of nations
will bow low before him.
And I will live for the Lord.*

(Ps 22:25, 26, 28, 31)

Jesus knew Psalm 22 by heart. He is praying it
in its entirety. He is expressing His total trust in the
Father's will. He knows that He will be raised from
the dead. He knows that His death is not an ultimate
defeat.

Nonetheless, the fact remains that the evangelist only gives the opening words of the psalm. This is not without meaning. Mark wants us to see Jesus abandoned and crushed in death. Like each of us, He faces the absurdity of death. There seems to be no sense nor victory in His suffering. His pain seems to have no obvious purpose. His first followers are scattered; His life is ended.

Only after Jesus breathes His last does Mark indicate the victory that His death has won. The temple veil is torn from top to bottom (15:38). God who has been the principal actor in the drama of Calvary now reveals His hand. He had spared Abraham from offering his son (Gen 22:11-14). He does not spare His own Son (Jn 3:16; Rom 8:32). God is using the suffering and death of Jesus to tear down every obstacle that separates us from himself. In the Crucified Jesus, all have access to God, Jew and Gentile alike (Eph 2:ll-22).

How appropriate, therefore, that at the moment of Jesus' death, the first confession of faith should be found on the lips of a pagan soldier. The man was a centurion. He had seen many die before, but never like this man. He exclaims:

Truly this man was the Son of God! (Mk 15:39)

At the very moment when death claims Him for its own, the hidden beauty of Jesus breaks forth in undeniable majesty. In His passion and death, the full mystery of Jesus is now revealed. Jesus is the Christ, the very Son of God!

"Behold, the man!"
(Jn 19:5)

CHAPTER 17

THE KING

And they placed over his head the written charge against him: This is Jesus, the King of the Jews. (Mt 27:37)

All four gospel writers tell us that, over the head of Jesus on the Cross, there was placed a sign that read, *"Jesus the Nazarene, the King of the Jews."* According to the fourth gospel, Pilate had this charge against Jesus written in three languages. In Latin, the language of human government and power. In Greek, the language of culture and wisdom. And, in Hebrew, the language of religion (Jn 19:19-20). The three greatest forces of the human spirit unconsciously acknowledged Him who is king not of just one people, but of all nations.

It was customary for the Romans to write the charge against a man condemned to death on a rough board in bold letters. On the way to the place of execution, two Roman soldiers would walk in front of the prisoner and two behind him. In front of this grim entourage, a man would carry the placard announcing the prisoner's crime. As Jesus made His way to Golgotha, word about the placard reached the Jewish rulers who had handed Jesus over to Pilate to crucify. They were infuriated. They could not bear to have anyone name Him "King of the Jews."

The chief priests were so hostile to Jesus that, even though they longed to be freed of Roman domination, they had claimed Caesar for their king in the trial before Pilate. They masked their hatred of Jesus beneath this sudden profession of loyalty to Rome. They wanted Jesus dead at all costs. Pilate was astute enough to understand their hypocrisy. Thus, to publically taunt these hypocrites, he issued his edict of condemnation: "Jesus the Nazarene, the King of the Jews." And he would not change it.

The Jerusalem elite recoiled at giving the title "king" to Jesus from Nazareth. *"What good could come from Nazareth?"* (Jn 1:46). Nazareth was a place not even mentioned in the entire Old Testament. This rural village in Galilee would hardly be the place from which would come the long-awaited Messiah-King. They vehemently sought Pilate to change the charge.

Pilate found no crime in Jesus. He was angry that he had been forced to do an injustice. Yet, the death of one individual was a small price to pay to avert the wrath of Caesar. Against the convictions of his own conscience, he had yielded to them once. He would not yield again. He responded, *"What I have written, I have written"* (Jn 19:22). In fact, Jesus will die not only as king of the Jews, but of all people.

The kingship of Christ is woven like a golden thread throughout the entire Passion narrative. In the trial before the members of the Sanhedrin, the chief priests question Jesus about the claim that He is the Messiah. The Jews expected the Messiah to be the Son of David, a royal figure who would cast off the yoke of Israel's oppressors. He would work miracles and establish God's kingdom on earth.

Before the questioning of these lawless judges, Jesus remains silent. *"Like a lamb led to slaughter or a sheep silent before shearers, he did not open his mouth"* (Is 53:7). The Incarnate Word wordless. Witnesses speak against Jesus. Their testimony is patently false. No grounds can be found to condemn Jesus (Mt 26:59-60). No lie, no falsehood, in thought, word, or deed can pass as truth in the presence of Jesus, then and now.

Caiaphas, the high priest, becomes annoyed at the slowness of the court to reach a guilty verdict. He knows of Jesus' public ministry. He is aware that many were hailing Jesus as the Messiah. Finally, in desperation, he puts Jesus under oath to answer whether or not He is "the Messiah, the Son of God."

Jesus knew that the people were expecting the Messiah to be a political figure. For this reason, throughout His public ministry, He carefully avoided claiming the title of Messiah. He did not wish to stir up the political unrest of His people.

Jesus heals a leper and then sternly warns him to remain silent (Mk 1:43). He raises Jairus' daughter from the dead and then strictly orders those present to tell no one (Mk 5:43). When Peter is the first to recognize Jesus as the Messiah, Jesus sternly warns Peter and all of the other apostles present *"not to tell anyone"* (Mk 8:30). After Peter, James, and John witness Jesus transfigured in glory, with Elijah and Moses pointing to Him as the Messiah, Jesus charges these three apostles *"not to relate what they had seen to anyone, except when the Son of Man had risen from the dead"* (Mk 9:9). Jesus enjoins silence on those who are privileged to recognize Him as Messiah.

Jesus avoids the Messianic enthusiasm of the people. If the people openly acknowledge Him as king, Rome would end His ministry as it did with the Jewish rebel Theudas and Judas the Galilean. After the multiplication of loaves and fish, when the crowds clamor to crown Him king, Jesus literally escapes and hides from them (Jn 6:15). He does not want to have His mission come to a premature end. Without prudence, courage is foolish.

However, at the end of His life, when the high priest puts Jesus under oath to say whether or not He is the Messiah, Jesus answers in no uncertain terms. Bound and held captive, Jesus is now free to speak. No danger at this point of His organizing a rebellion against Rome. No fear that He would command an army as the Messiah that many were expecting. In response to Caiaphas' question if He is the Messiah, Jesus solemnly proclaims:

*I am; and you will see the Son of Man seated
at the right hand of the Power and coming
with the clouds of heaven.* (Mk 14:62)

In his majestic "I am," Jesus answers both parts
of the high priest's question. He is the Messiah. He
is the Son of God. And, then with great dignity, He
proclaims that He will be the final judge and those
condemning Him will stand before His tribunal.
These judges, now blinded by their self-interest, are
going to see Him return in glory as the Son of Man.
Self-interest is always the enemy of truth and compassion.

Caiaphas had asked Jesus if He was the Messiah-
King. His line of questioning followed the popular
understanding of a political Messiah. In responding,
Jesus goes far beyond the expectations of His day.
He cites the passage about the mysterious Son of
Man who comes at the end of time and establishes
God's reign over the whole world (Dan 7:14). In
effect, He lays claim not to political power as a king,
but to divine authority as the very Son of God. He
equates himself with God.

At this very moment in the trial of Jesus before
the chief priests, Peter who had first confessed Jesus
as Messiah is on the outside of the courtroom, shud-
dering in the cold. Fearful for his own life, he denies
Jesus three times. Inside the courtroom, Jesus, with
no fear for His life, makes the clearest assertion of

His divinity. Not only is He the Messiah, He is God! From this point on, the outcome is clear.

For the Jews who were strict monotheists, Jesus' claim is blasphemy. He must die. He cannot be their divine king. Only the one, true God is. They condemn Him to death. The highest truths can become servants of the lowliest deeds when our hearts are hardened and our eyes blinded by self-interest. So many crimes continue to be done in the name of religion. True religion never breeds hate, only love, never death, only life.

In Jewish law, blasphemy deserved the death penalty (Lev 24:16). Since the Jews could not impose the death penalty, they bring Jesus to Pilate to have Him condemned to death. It is the day before the Passover. As is the custom, Pilate carries out his judicial function, beginning at 5 a.m. The chief priests present the only charge that would merit the death penalty in Pilate's eyes. Jesus is a threat to the power of Rome. Thus, they accuse Jesus as claiming to be a king.

Pilate is a realist. The Passover feast was a time of great national expectations. If Jesus is truly, as they say, a king, He is a threat to Rome and must be done away with immediately. In responding to Pilate, Jesus proclaims His kingship. But, He distances himself from the popular notion of kingship. He tells Pilate, *"If my kingdom did belong to this world, my attendants would be fighting to keep me from being handed over to the Jews. But as it is, my kingdom is not here"* (Jn 18:36). The kingship of Christ is the reign of truth, justice, and peace that come from above and cannot be imposed by human force.

Finding Jesus innocent of any kind of political kingship, Pilate appeals to the human sympathy of Jesus' accusers. He has Jesus taken away and scourged. A cowardly compromise. So brutal was Roman scourging prior to execution that some individuals died before they could be crucified. Others went mad.

Jesus is stripped, tied to a pillar, and scourged with leather straps with sharp pieces of bone attached. His skin torn, His body drenched in His own blood, the soldiers make sport of Him. They robe Him in a purple cloak and place a reed in His hand as a scepter. They mock Him, laughing and hailing Him as "King of the Jews" (Jn 19:5). They are young men, looking for some diversion from their hard military routine at the expense of another. How often inexperienced youth needs time to understand the pain of life in another.

The soldiers drive a crown of thorns into Jesus' head (Mk 15:16-20). Thorns came with the curse. They sprung from the earth because of Adam and Eve's transgression (Gen 3:18). Now the New Adam wears thorns. As the curse began with thorns, it ends with thorns. The New Adam is making restitution for us all. Next, the soldiers give their homage to their newly-crowned king. They kneel. They spit. They strike His head. They fill the praetorium with their laughter. Jesus truly is a king in humility and suffering.

When Jesus is brought back to Pilate, he finds no guilt in Him. He is afraid to do the right and hesitant to do the wrong. Yet, out of fear of losing his own position, he stains his judgment seat with innocent blood and hands Jesus over to His enemies to be crucified with the words, *"Here is your King"* (Jn 19:14). Beneath the cruel sport of the soldiers and the sarcasm of Pilate, the truth neither could discern: Jesus is a king.

CHAPTER 18

THE KINGDOM COME

For behold, the kingdom of God is among you.
(Lk 17:21)

On the Cross, Jesus truly dies as king. Mark tells us that they "brought" Jesus to Golgotha. The Greek root word for "brought" (φερειν) means, "to bear or to carry some burden." Luke uses this word when telling us that Simon of Cyrene was made to "carry" the Cross of Jesus (Lk 23:26). So weak has Jesus become from the brutal scourging at the hands of the soldiers that He himself has to be dragged to Golgotha while Simon carries the Cross for Him.

Before nailing Jesus to the Cross, the soldiers offered Him wine drugged with myrrh. A common custom offered by these stolid executioners. Or perhaps a small act of compassion in the midst of untold cruelty. The drug was to help the crucified lose consciousness and thus suffer less in dying. But Jesus refuses to take it (Mk 15:23). This seemingly small notice is of great significance.

In Proverbs, the queen mother tells her son Lemuel, king of Massa, that the common criminal should take wine in the moment of suffering to forget his misery. But, she warns him:

It is not for kings, Lemuel, not for kings to drink wine; strong drink is not for princes, lest in drinking they forget what has been decreed, and violate the rights of any who are in need.

(Prv 31:4-5)

Since Jesus is king, He refuses to be drugged. He will accept His death with all His faculties intact. On the Cross, He is the king giving true judgment to the world.

On His way to Jerusalem for the last week of His life, Salome, the mother of James and John had asked Jesus that her two sons sit one on His right and one on His left when He established His kingdom (Mt 20:21). Both James and John were close to Jesus. Not only were they His cousins, but, along with Peter, they were part of His inner circle. Jesus allowed them to witness both the raising of Jairus' daughter from the dead and His own transfiguration in glory. Salome's request, therefore, does not appear unwarranted.

Furthermore, Salome was the wife of Zebedee, a man of some wealth. As one of the women who accompanied Jesus during His public ministry and provided for His needs (Mt 27:55-56), she may have felt emboldened to make a request for her two sons. How often we make the mistake in thinking what we give to the Lord obliges Him to do our will!

The mother of James and John misunderstood the kingship of Jesus. As many who were following

Jesus, she was expecting Jesus to inaugurate His kingdom on earth. He had already shown His power through His many miracles, healings, and exorcisms. Soon, she reasoned, He would usher in His reign on earth with great glory. For her sons to sit on the right and left hand of Jesus would be the highest honor.

There is only one other time when Matthew speaks of one person on the right and another on the left of Jesus. It is at the crucifixion. There two thieves are crucified one on Jesus' right and the other on His left (Mt 27:38). The mother of James and John is present with the other faithful women. She sees and begins to realize that this is the moment in which Jesus is ushering in His kingdom. Salome had asked for earthly honor for her sons. Jesus is opening the way to eternal glory for them and all who believe in Him.

The thief on the right of Jesus is moved by Jesus' nobility. Despite His intense agony, Jesus does not curse; He blesses. He does not condemn; He forgives. In the most audacious cry of one dying man to another, the thief cries out:

Lord, remember me when you come into your kingdom. (Lk 23:42)

With the eyes of faith, he acknowledges the deepest truth about Jesus. Jesus is truly a king.

From the first day of His public ministry, Jesus had preached the coming of the kingdom of God (Mk 1:14-15). What Jesus meant by "the kingdom of God," He revealed in giving us the Our Father.

The second petition of the Our Father is two parallel lines: *"Thy kingdom come. Thy will be done on earth as it is in heaven"* (Mt 6:10). Typical of Hebrew poetry, the second phrase is parallel to the first phrase. It repeats it, expands it and explains its meaning. Thus, for Jesus, the kingdom of God is not a geographical territory, a nation or people under a theocracy. Rather, it is that state or condition where God's will is perfectly done. It is the rule or the sovereignty of God over His creation and all people.

At times, Jesus spoke of the kingdom of God as a present reality. In responding to His adversaries who demanded proof of His mission, Jesus offered His exorcism of an evil spirit from a mute man as the sign that *"the kingdom of God has come"* (Lk 11:20). When the Pharisees asked Jesus to tell them when the kingdom would come, He simply replied, *"Behold, the kingdom of God is among you"* (Lk 17:21).

In Jesus' ministry, the kingdom of God was truly present. And only those who totally depended on God were entering it (Mk 10:15). And, so it is today. Only when we allow God to have dominion over our hearts and souls, only when we submit our thoughts, words, deeds, and actions to His law of love do we enter His kingdom.

After Peter confesses Jesus to be the Messiah, Jesus instructs His disciples on the necessity of the Cross. And, then He says to them:

Amen, I say to you, there are some standing here who will not taste death until they see that the kingdom of God has come in power.
(Mk 9:1)

In a word, Jesus acknowledges that the kingdom, though present in His ministry, had not fully come. We are heirs to the sin of our first parents. Adam and Eve did not obey God nor do we. As Paul teaches:

Through the disobedience of one person, the many were made sinners. (Rom 5:19)

We are far from the moment when each of us consistently and always does the will of God. Our obedience to God is not perfect. The spirit of rebellion, that deep-seated desire for independence from God, lurks beneath our best intentions. We long to place our hearts totally in God's hands. Yet, we do not. For this reason, Jesus speaks of the kingdom as yet to come. And, so we pray, "Thy kingdom come."

At the Last Supper, Jesus institutes the Eucharist as the memorial of His upcoming death and Resurrection. And, then He says:

Amen, I say to you, I shall not drink again the fruit of the vine until the day when I drink it new in the kingdom of God. (Mk 14:25)

Jesus is looking forward at this point beyond His death to the eschatological banquet when the kingdom has come in its fullness. And, it is by His dying on the Cross that Jesus accomplishes this.

At the moment before Jesus expires, He utters a loud cry (Mt 27:50; Mk 15:37; Lk 23:46). This is not the cry of an anguished man gasping in relief. It is not the pitiful cry of a helpless victim giving up in despair. It is something more profound.

A crucified man died completely spent. But, not Jesus. He has strength enough to utter this loud cry. The fourth evangelist tells us that Jesus actually cries out at this moment the words *"It is finished"* (Jn 19:30). In Greek, it is just one word (τετέλεσται). It is the shortest of all the words spoken by Jesus on the Cross. But, in it is contained the whole meaning of Jesus' mission. Jesus had once told His disciples:

> *My food is to do the will of the one who sent me and to finish his work.* (Jn 4:34)

In dying, He brings to completion God's work. He perfectly fulfills the Father's will, *"becoming obedient, even to death on the cross"* (Phil 2:8) and ushers in the kingdom of God in power.

In recording Jesus' death, all four evangelists do not say *"he died."* Matthew says *"he released his spirit"* (Mt 27:50). Mark and Luke say *"he breathed his last"* (Mk 15:41; Lk 23:46). John says *"he handed over his spirit"* (Jn 19:30). They use words to indicate that Jesus remains master of His life to the end. With His work complete, Jesus summons death as His servant. He has closed the sad chapter of Adam's sin. He is now opening a new chapter of grace.

Therefore, returning to the Father, Jesus cries out in a loud voice. It is the shout of triumph. It is the cry of the Conqueror claiming victory. The battle is over. The strife is won. Sin is defeated. Death overcome. From Jesus' pierced heart, grace is given us in abundance to do God's will.

In dying, Jesus embodies in His very person the kingdom of God. His obedience to the Father establishes the absolute sovereignty of God over all creation. Through Christ and in Him, we enter the kingdom and we are saved. Purpled in His own blood and crowned with thorns, Christ reigns from the Cross. The kingdom of God has come in power and Christ is King of all time and all peoples.

God raised this Jesus; of this we are all witnesses. Exalted at the right hand of God, he received the promise of the Holy Spirit from the Father and poured it forth, as you (both) see and hear. (Acts 2:32-33)

CONCLUSION

From a merely human point of view, the Passion is a loss; the Resurrection, the gain; the Cross, a humiliation; the empty grave, the exaltation. As we have seen, this is not the perspective of the gospel writers. They write their accounts because the Crucified Jesus is the Risen Lord. They proclaim His suffering and death as the way to glory. They show these events themselves as victory.

The Passion Story has power. Jesus abandoned by His disciples challenges us to a deeper union with God in Christ even when this entails separation from others. No human love is worthy of the name that leads away from Love itself. Mary standing at the foot of the Cross reminds us that fidelity is possible. Personal struggle is no reason to lose hope. We already have been made sharers in the new life of grace as members of Jesus' family *"born, not of blood nor of the will of the flesh nor of the will of man, but of God"* (Jn 1:12-13).

Suffering is part of the fabric of this creation (Rom 8:12-25). Not even God's own Son was spared its pain. Far from dulling our minds to the world as we live in it, the Passion narrative exposes the world in all its brutal pain. In remaining true to himself and to His Father in the midst of suffering, Jesus revealed His true identity and ours as well.

The Resurrection does not remove pain from our lives. It enables us to follow Jesus along the *Via Crucis*. Jesus Crucified shows us that God's purpose works quietly not only in sunshine but even in rain. God has a purpose in suffering. Through suffering which God allows to enter our lives, He is leading us, His sons and daughters, to glory.

It would be indeed a great mistake to represent the Christian life as easy. It is not! Many a cross is of our own doing. At times, we suffer the dread consequences of our sinful deeds. Yet, at other times we suffer because of our goodness. Through fidelity to God's will in all things, great and small, we are made holy.

The pennant at the masthead is a small thing. Yet it shows plainly the way the wind is blowing. A look, a word, a sigh, a gesture when in accord with God's love, despite the struggle, clearly show the direction of our life. And, though we fail at times, we need never despair. Through the transforming power of the Cross, even our failures may become successes. When we join our lives to Christ Crucified, God takes the emptiness of our broken life and lets stream in the joy of Easter morn.

When Jesus stepped up from the Jordan River freshly drenched with the Father's blessing, the world was not ready for Him. His coming contradicted the world's thoughts and actions. When we emerge from the waters of Baptism as sons and daughters of God, we face the world's opposition to the Christian way of life. Simon of Cyrene who helped Jesus carry the Cross is no mythical figure. He is each one of us called to share in the sufferings of Jesus. We are called to say with Paul:

Now I rejoice in my sufferings for your sake, and in my flesh I am filling up what is lacking in the afflictions of Christ on behalf of his body, which is the church. (Col 1:24)

Patience and perseverance are part of the Christian path. At times, we may stumble in the darkness, groping for the light. We do not reach the truth or come to perfect love in one step. Each evangelist realized this. Each took the traditions of the believing community and, under the inspiration of the Holy Spirit, re-told them in his own way. Their example invites us to do the same. Moved by the Holy Spirit who dwells within us, we are called to re-tell the Passion of Jesus with our lives. For in so doing, we experience the richness of God's love; and, we ourselves become evangelists, "bearers of good news." To a waiting world, we are witnesses to the saving power of the Cross.

Heavenly Father, You delivered Your Son to the Death of the Cross to save us from evil.

Scriptural Way of the Cross

The Way of the Cross is a devotion to the Sacred Passion, in which we accompany, in spirit, our Blessed Lord in His sorrowful journey from the house of Pilate to Calvary. As we pray this devotion, we recall to mind, with sorrow and love, all that took place from the time when He was condemned to death to His being laid in the tomb. There are fourteen Stations, or places, in the Way of the Cross, at which something took place. At each Station we should say the Our Father, the Hail Mary, and the Glory Be with love and sorrow for our sins, meditating on the suffering of our Lord represented to us at the Station.

Opening Prayer

HEAVENLY Father, grant that we who meditate on the Passion and Death of Your Son, Jesus Christ, may imitate in our lives His love and self-giving to You and to others. We ask this through Christ our Lord.

1. Jesus Is Condemned to Death

Jn 3:16f; Is 53:7; Jn 15:13

O Jesus, help me to appreciate Your
sanctifying grace more and more.

GOD so loved the world that He gave His only Son, . . . to save the world through Him.

He was harshly treated, yet He submitted and did not open His mouth. He was silent like a lamb led to the slaughter or a sheep before the shearers, and did not open His mouth.

No one has greater love than this: to lay down one's life for one's friends.

Let us pray.

Father, in the flesh of Your Son You condemned sin. Grant us the gift of eternal life in the same Christ our Lord.

2. Jesus Bears His Cross

Is 53:4; Lk 9:23; Mt 11:28f

O Jesus, You chose to die for me. Help me
to love You always with all my heart.

SURELY, He took up our infirmities and carried our sorrows.

Those who wish to be My followers must deny their very selves, take up their cross daily, and follow Me.

Take My yoke upon you and learn from Me, . . . for My yoke is easy and My burden is light.

Let us pray.

Father, Your Son Jesus humbled Himself and became obedient to death. Teach us to glory above all else in the Cross, in which is our salvation. Grant this through Christ our Lord.

3. Jesus Falls the First Time

Lam 3:16f; Is 53:6; Jn 1:29

O Jesus, make me strong to conquer my wicked passions, and to rise quickly from sin.

HE has broken My teeth with gravel and trampled Me in the dust. I have been deprived of peace and have forgotten what happiness is.

The Lord has laid upon Him the iniquity of us all.

Behold the Lamb of God Who takes away the sin of the world.

Let us pray.

Father, help us to remain irreproachable in Your sight, so that we can offer You our body as a holy and living offering. We ask this in the Name of Jesus the Lord.

4. Jesus Meets His Mother

Lk 2:49; Lam 1:12; Jn 16:22

O Jesus, grant me a tender love for Your
Mother, who offered You for love of me.

DID you not know that I must be in My Father's house? Come, all you who pass along the road, look and see whether there is any pain like My pain.

You are now in anguish, but I will see you again. Then your hearts will rejoice, and no one shall deprive you of your joy.

Let us pray.

Father, accept the sorrows of the Blessed Virgin Mary, Mother of Your Son. May they obtain from Your mercy every good for our salvation. Grant this through Christ our Lord.

5. Jesus Is Helped by Simon

Mt 25:40; Gal 6:2; Jn 13:16

O Jesus, like Simon lead me ever closer to
You through my daily crosses and trials.

WHATEVER you did for one of the least of these brothers and sisters of Mine, you did for Me.

Bear one another's burdens, and in this way you will fulfill the law of Christ. A servant is not greater than his master.

Let us pray.

Father, You have first loved us and You sent Your Son to expiate our sins. Grant that we may love one another and bear each other's burdens. We ask this through Christ our Lord.

6. Veronica Wipes the Face of Jesus

Is 52:14; Jn 14:9; Heb 1:3

O Jesus, imprint Your image on my heart
that I may be faithful to You all my life.

HIS appearance was disfigured beyond that of any man, and His form marred beyond human likeness.

Whoever has seen Me has seen the Father.

The Son is the reflection of God's glory and the exact representation of His very being.

Let us pray.

Heavenly Father, grant that we may reflect Your Son's glory and be transformed into His image so that we may be configured to Him. We ask this in the Name of Jesus.

7. Jesus Falls a Second Time

Ps 118:13; Heb 4:15; Mt 11:28

O Jesus, I repent for having offended You.
Grant me forgiveness of all my sins.

I WAS hard pressed and close to falling, but the Lord came to My aid.

We do not have a High Priest Who is unable to sympathize with our weaknesses, but One Who has been tested in every way as we are, but without sinning.

Come to Me, all you who are weary and overburdened, and I will give you rest.

Let us pray.

God our Father, grant that we may walk in the footsteps of Jesus Who suffered for us and redeemed us not with gold and silver but with the price of His own blood. We ask this through Christ our Lord.

8. Jesus Speaks to the Women

Lk 23:28; Jn 15:6; Lk 13:3

O Jesus, grant me tears of compassion for
Your sufferings and of sorrow for my sins.

DAUGHTERS of Jerusalem, do not weep for Me. Weep rather for yourselves and for your children.

Whoever does not abide in Me will be thrown away like a withered branch.

You will all come to the same end [as some Galileans who perished] unless you repent.

Let us pray.

Heavenly Father, You desire to show mercy rather than anger toward all who hope in You. Grant that we may weep for our sins and merit the grace of Your glory. We ask this in the Name of Jesus the Lord.

9. **Jesus Falls a Third Time**

Ps 22:15f; Phil 2:5-7; Lk 14:11

O Jesus, let me never yield to despair. Let me come to You in hardship and spiritual distress.

MY strength is trickling away like water, and all My bones are dislocated. My heart has turned to wax and melts within Me. My mouth is as dry as clayware, and My tongue sticks to My jaws; You have laid Me down in the dust of death.

Let your attitude be identical to that of Christ: . . . He emptied Himself, taking the form of a slave.

All who exalt themselves shall be humbled, and those who humble themselves shall be exalted.

Let us pray.

God our Father, look with pity on us oppressed by the weight of our sins and grant us Your forgiveness. Help us to serve You with our whole heart. We ask this through Christ our Lord.

10. Jesus Is Stripped of His Garments

Ps 22:19; Lk 14:33; Rom 13:14

O Jesus, let me sacrifice all my attachments
rather than imperil the divine life of my soul.

THEY divide My garments among them, and for My clothing they cast lots.

Those who do not renounce all their possessions cannot be My disciples.

Put on the Lord Jesus Christ and allow no opportunity for the flesh to gratify its sinful desires.

Let us pray.

Heavenly Father, let nothing deprive us of Your love—neither trials nor distress nor persecution. May we become the wheat of Christ and be one pure bread. Grant this through Christ our Lord.

11. Jesus Is Nailed to the Cross

Ps 22:17f; Lk 23:34; Jn 6:38

O Jesus, strengthen my faith and increase my love
for You. Help me to accept my crosses.

THEY have pierced My hands and My feet; I can count all My bones.

Father, forgive them; for they do not know what they are doing.

I have come down from heaven not to do My own Will but the Will of Him Who sent Me.

Let us pray.

Heavenly Father, Your Son reconciled us to You and to one another. Help us to embrace His gift of grace and remain united with You. We ask this through Christ our Lord.

12. Jesus Dies on the Cross

Jn 12:32; Lk 23:46; Phil 2:8-9

O Jesus, I thank You for making me a child of God.
Help me to forgive others.

WHEN I am lifted up from the earth, I will draw everyone to Myself.

Father, into Your hands I commend My spirit.

He humbled Himself and became obedient to death, even death on a Cross! Because of this, God greatly exalted Him.

Let us pray.

God our Father, by His Death Your Son has conquered death, and by His Resurrection He has given us life. Help us to adore His Death and embrace His Life. Grant this in the Name of Jesus the Lord.

13. Jesus Is Taken Down from the Cross
Lk 24:26; Ps 119:165; 1 Jn 4:9f

O Jesus, through the intercession of Your holy
Mother, let me be pleasing to You.

THUS it is written that the Messiah would suffer and on the third day rise from the dead.

Those who love Your law have great peace.

This is how God showed His love: He sent His only Son to the world . . . as an atoning sacrifice for our sins.

Let us pray.

God our Father, grant that we may be associated in Christ's Death so that we may advance toward the Resurrection with great hope. We ask this through Christ our Lord.

14. Jesus Is Placed in the Tomb
Jn 12:24; Rom 6:10-11; 1 Cor 15:4

O Jesus, strengthen my will to live for You on earth
and bring me to eternal bliss in heaven.

UNLESS a grain of wheat falls into the earth and dies, it remains just a grain of wheat. However, if it dies, it bears much fruit.

When Christ died, He died to sin, once and for all. However, the life He lives, He lives for God. In the same way, you must regard yourselves as being dead to sin and alive for God in Christ Jesus.

Christ . . . was raised to life on the third day in accordance with the Scriptures.

Let us pray.

Heavenly Father, You raised Jesus from the dead through Your Holy Spirit. Grant life to our mortal bodies through that same Spirit Who abides in us. We ask this in the Name of Jesus the Lord.

Concluding Prayer

HEAVENLY Father, You delivered Your Son to the Death of the Cross to save us from evil. Grant us the grace of the Resurrection. We ask this through Christ our Lord.

THE WAY OF THE CROSS — By St. Alphonsus Liguori. This booklet is a devotion to the Sacred Passion of our Lord. We follow Him from when He was condemned to death to His being laid in the tomb. 32 pages. Size 3^7/8 x 6^1/4.

No. 14/05—Flexible cover............................ **.95**
ISBN 978-0-89942-014-1
Also Available in Spanish: El Camino de la Cruz
No. 16/S ISBN 978-0-89942-016-5 .... **.95**

THROUGH HIS WOUNDS WE ARE HEALED — By Vojtěch Kodet, O. Carm. This brief but profound book helps us to more fully understand how the Way of the Cross can be a wonderful means of uniting ourselves and the difficulties in our lives more intimately with Christ and His sufferings. 64 pages. Size 4 x 6^1/4.

No. 116/04—Flexible cover...................... **3.95**
ISBN 978-0-89942-116-2

LIVING WITH HOPE — By Cardinal Carlo Maria Martini, S.J. Reflecting on the author's pastoral thoughts on the actions and teachings of Jesus and the Church will help us to live in Christian hope and proclaim this hope to others. 192 pages. Size 5^1/4 x 7^3/4.

No. 167/04—Flexible cover...................... **8.95**
ISBN 978-1-937913-78-6

DAILY MEDITATIONS WITH THE HOLY SPIRIT — By Rev. Jude Winkler, OFM Conv. Through daily Scripture readings and prayer, Fr. Winkler offers us an opportunity to develop a closer relationship with the Holy Spirit and to apply the fruits of our meditation to our everyday lives. 192 pages. Size 4 x 6¼.

No. 198/19—Dura-Lux cover................... **8.95**
ISBN 978-1-937913-56-4

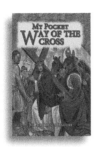

MY POCKET WAY OF THE CROSS — by St. Alphonsus Liguori. With glorious full-color illustrations, this pocket- or purse-size book offers those who wish to pray the Stations a handy companion for this popular devotion on the Sacred Passion of Our Lord. 48 pages. Size 2¹/₂ x 3³/₄.

No. 18/04—Flexible cover **1.25**
ISBN 978-1-937913-30-4

THE LITANY OF THE SACRED HEART — By Mario Collantes. This collection of 33 invocations with accompanying commentaries offers a meaningful way to express and nurture our love for the Person of Jesus, Who is the Source of our salvation and hope. Full color. 96 pages. Size 4³/₈ x 6³/₄.

No. 374/04—Flexible cover **5.95**
ISBN 978-0-89942-366-1

JOYFULLY LIVING THE GOSPEL DAY BY DAY — By Rev. John Catoir. Each day contains a specific Scripture quotation, reflection, and prayer to encourage joyous participation in the Christian life. 192 pages. Size 4 x 6¹/₄.

No. 188/19—Dura-Lux cover **8.95**
ISBN 978-1-937913-04-5

THE IMITATION OF CHRIST — by Thomas à Kempis. Prayer book size edition. This treasured book has brought peace to readers for many ages by showing how to follow the life of Christ to which all are called. Includes a full-color Rosary and Stations of the Cross section. 288 pages. Size 4 x 6¹/₄.

No. 320/19—Dura-Lux cover **9.95**
ISBN 978-1-941243-16-9

FROM THE CROSS TO THE EMPTY TOMB

Most Rev. Arthur J. Serratelli, S.T.D., S.S.L., D.D.

As Christians, we make our life-journey in union with Christ Crucified. The *Via Crucis* is the school

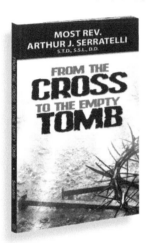

of Christian life. As Peter once asked Jesus, the world questions each of us today, "*Quo Vadis*?" "Where are you going?" It will help each of us respond to this question by accompanying Jesus on the Way to the Cross. I offer the following brief meditations on individuals who were with Jesus in the last hours of His own life on earth.

—From the Author's Introduction

The author invites you to journey with those who were with Jesus in His last hours. You may be like Peter one day, and like Judas, Simon, Mary Magdalene, or Our Lady on another. This Lenten book provides a deeper appreciation for God's eternal saving love. 96 pages. Size 4³/₈ x 6³/₄.

No. 928/04—Flexible cover **5.95**
ISBN 978-1-947070-13-4

THE SEVEN GIFTS
OF THE HOLY SPIRIT

Most Rev. Arthur J. Serratelli, S.T.D., S.S.L., D.D.

Jesus alone possessed the seven gifts of the Holy Spirit in their fullness. But, the Holy Spirit graciously gives those same gifts to all who follow Jesus.

The seven gifts are our inheritance as baptized and confirmed Christians. We do not earn them. We do not merit them. They are given to us gratuitously. They make us open to the promptings of the Holy Spirit in our lives. They help us grow in holiness, making us fit for heaven. These seven gifts of the Holy Spirit help us live a truly authentic Christian way of life.

—From the Author's Introduction

Through history, art, Scripture, and Catholic documents, you will appreciate and grasp more fully how the seven gifts of the Holy Spirit can help you to live a truly authentic Christian life filled with peace and joy. 96 pages. Size 4³/₈ x 6³/₄.

No. 930/04—Flexible cover **5.95**

ISBN 978-1-947070-23-3

Bishop Arthur J. Serratelli is the seventh bishop of the Diocese of Paterson, N.J. He is at present second-term chairman of the International Commission on English in the Liturgy; member of the Vatican's Congregation of Divine Worship and the Discipline of the Sacraments; member of Vox Clara; and chairman for the Vatican's Dialogue between the Catholic Church and the World Alliance of Baptists. Formerly, he was a Professor of Sacred Scripture and Systematics. He has served a three-year term as chairman of the Committee for the Translation of Sacred Scripture of the United States Conference of Catholic Bishops; twice chairman of the Committee on Divine Worship of the United States Conference of Catholic Bishops; chairman of the Committee on Doctrine; and member of the Subcommittee for the Review of Catechetical Texts.

The Bishop's first book is *From the Cross to the Empty Tomb,* and his second one is titled *The Seven Gifts of the Holy Spirit.*